Simon and Schuster   New York

Plants That *Really* Bloom Indoors

George and Virginie Elbert

Illustrated by Helen Matsubu

Copyright © 1974 by George and Virginie Elbert
All rights reserved
including the right of reproduction
in whole or in part in any form
Published by Simon and Schuster
Rockefeller Center, 630 Fifth Avenue
New York, New York 10020

Designed by Elizabeth Woll
Manufactured in the United States of America
Printed by the Murray Printing Company
Bound by American Book–Stratford Press

2   3   4   5   6   7   8   9   10

Library of Congress Cataloging in Publication Data

Elbert, George, 1911–
    Plants that really bloom indoors.

    1. House plants.   2. Flowers.   I. Elbert, Virginie,
joint author.   II. Title.
SB419.E42   635.9'65   74–9890
ISBN 0–671–21797–6

To SUZANNE

Contents

The Great House Plant Breakthrough

In the last few years sensational progress has been made in adapting ornamental plants, formerly grown only in greenhouses or in the garden, to the house. It started around 1938 with the marketing of the first fluorescent lamps and the discovery that plants can be grown and bloomed successfully under artificial light. This stimulated worldwide exploration for plants particularly suitable for the new method. And, as more and more were found for the light garden, the windowsill and sun-porch gardener also benefited.

Although fluorescent light was the principal cause for this change, there were others. Large-capacity room humidifiers, soilless mediums, specialized chemical fertilizers, plastic pots and trays, even the popularity of air conditioning, made it easier to grow blooming plants in the home than ever before.

We have just looked through an indoor gardening book published in 1946. Many authors at that time really raised their plants in greenhouses but called anything which would stay in flower for a while indoors a house plant. But this author was very honest and included in his list only those which really could live in his home. It consisted mainly of flowering bulbs, with a nod to the growing popularity of the African Violet. All the plants except that one were strictly seasonal bloomers. It is difficult to realize today how happy gardeners were to achieve a few weeks of flowering after a year of care.

Of course, we still do raise the seasonal plants, but they are rapidly losing their former importance. We have included a number of them because they are beautiful and because our modern repertory does not yet quite satisfy the need for a wide range of choices. But even these seasonal plants can grow far better than formerly.

So much has the situation changed that most of the tropical foliage plants are no longer a serious challenge to the grower either on the windowsill or in the light garden. We can maintain the big plants in any corner of a house or an apartment by means of a simple floodlight. Many which were once displayed in botanic gardens as rarities can be bought in ordinary plant shops. You can see them growing in apartments, building lobbies and offices.

Blooming plants, however, are still a real challenge. They require more light and more care than foliage plants. Nevertheless more and more people will accept the challenge, since flowering plants are so much more dynamic and colorful. While foliage plants are rather static and have a tendency to become merely a piece of green furniture, flowering plants have distinctive personalities. We become far more attached to them and soon treat them almost like animal pets. Observing a plant bursting into bloom in the home is a new and exciting experience. Suddenly we have the makings of a garden indoors and we become aware of its contribution to the good life. It is hard to exaggerate the importance of this amenity for people living in the city or in a crowded suburb. As for those who live in the country, the potential has been created of carrying gardening right through the winter. October no longer marks the end of gardening but the beginning of a different and equally exciting horticultural experience.

The new plants are all of tropical origin because they are particularly suited to indoor conditions. With modern equipment, homes provide an environment very close to, and in some ways superior to, that of a greenhouse. Our new plants are an esthetic experience. For those who have spent their gardening years outdoors growing zinnias, marigolds and petunias, plus a few other standbys *ad infinitum*, their beauty is a revelation. Most of them can be grown rather small to fit confined spaces, but if encouraged to reach their full potential, they can become spectacular specimen plants. Amateurs, with the space to do it, raise huge pots and baskets of Columneas, Aeschynanthus, Hypocyrtas, orchids, bromeliads and Begonias in the house. These plants are now winning the highest awards at the spring flower shows, where outdoor plants formerly reigned supreme.

Fluorescent light has been largely responsible for the discovery that plants can be truly everblooming indoors. It was a rule of the old horticulture that they must have a seasonal rest coupled with the belief that they can "bloom themselves to death." Under the uniform light and temperature conditions of our homes, certain plants disprove both theories by flowering continuously, day after day, throughout the year.

If you think something is impossible you will not attempt it. Breeders once believed that the most bloom to be hoped for was off and on through the year, or for a period of a few months. It did not seem possible to hybridize for truly continuous bloom. But once convinced that it could be done, they went to work. Many of the new plants are selections or hybridizations resulting from a real effort to extend the blooming period with the object of a complete annual cycle. And this has meant not only a search for new plants for long bloom but also reexamination of the feasibility of improving the old ones.

Everbloom is very desirable. But if this escapes us, most of us will settle for winter flowering. In summer, we are away from home more, or are gardening outdoors. Plants are more neglected at that time of year, the solution being, where possible, to set them out-of-doors and let nature take care of them. But we do very much want winter bloom and will naturally favor plants which perform at that time.

All the plants we list have been successfully grown and bloomed by us or by other amateur horticulturists whose methods and results we have had the opportunity to observe. You will find some of the old plants here as well as the new; hopefully the choices are balanced between the two. Many varieties are really so new that every scrap of information about them is important and of practical use.

The wealth of plant materials which is flooding in on us is so great that we are still unable to give specific directions for most of them. Our new technology has not only encouraged introductions from tropical lands but has created a new potential for many hundreds of plants which have already been cultivated in greenhouses but rarely in the home. The orchid family offers a host of treasures but is still relatively unexplored territory for the indoor grower. He just has not had the time to try out the whole gamut of possibilities, eliminating the failures and promoting the successful plants. Ultimately this one family will offer hundreds, perhaps thousands, of plants with a bewildering number of forms and colors for the indoor garden.

Most familiar is the gesneriad family because, from the very beginning, some have been house plants. When the big surge started, it was to this family that amateurs turned their particular attention. The results have been astonishing. In some ten years the numbers of species in cultivation has doubled and hybridization has gone hand in hand. Every year brings us new plants. And with more people growing them in the home, we are learning more about them. When the easier orchids become equally popular we will be able to grow more of the others to perfection. The same rule applies to other families. Gradually we will build up enough basic cultural knowledge to deal with many families and a host of individual species and cultivars.

The plants which we describe in greater detail are those we consider the best and easiest for the indoor grower. Related species and cultivars should be tried by those who have learned the fundamentals. The intermediate and expert growers can bloom a great many other plants. We have only indicated a few of these possibilities but, as soon as you feel you have the capability, you too should experiment. You will be surprised and delighted with the richness of the repertory.

What we have written above is really a justification for this book. The time has come for one devoted entirely to blooming plants in the house. A person can very well garden outdoors with but a rudimentary knowledge of horticulture. The fool-proof seeds are bought, planted and left to take care of themselves. Nature does the work. But in the house *you* create the environment and you are the only "nature" the plant will ever know. So it is up to you to learn how to do the job. Good growing.

Part 1

Basic Culture
for Blooming Plants

How Tropical Plants Grow

In their native habitats tropical house plants exist mostly under two very different conditions. If they grow in the ground, the soil is subjected to the effect of enormous rainfalls which leaches out any nutriment it might have originally contained. They live on little else than sun, water and humidity plus the fall of debris from taller vegetation. The soil is wet most of the time, and compacted. A lighter soil and better nutrition is required in the house.

The other kinds grow either in debris on branches in the trees of the forest or in more organic situations on the ground, such as anthills or piles of detritus which have accumulated in one place. These growing mediums are fibrous, moisture-retaining but well aerated. They are low in nutrition but better than the leached-out ground soil. This is very different from garden loam and, though it is true that the addition of humus and compost approximates the above desirable conditions, we can do this far more easily by other means.

SOIL Modern house plant growing has changed many of the old ways. "Garden loam" is definitely out, along with all those messes of compost, humus, manure, sand, etc., which were formerly favored for exotic plants and made indoor horticulture so deliciously "organic." Excellent results could and still can be achieved through these means, but they involve a lot of work, great care, and specialized knowledge, in order to compound the right mixtures which not everybody has or needs to know about.

All soils used in the *house* must be sterilized. Organic life in soil is fine if it is of the useful kind, and deadly if it is a nuisance or a pest. Natural soil contains both types and there is no way of being kind to the beneficial organisms while killing off the bad ones. Sterilization in the home oven—about the only place available—is a chore.

Even sterilized garden soil usually lacks a lot of the qualities desirable in a house plant mix. It is much too heavy, dries out too rapidly and, most of the time, its chemical makeup is unknown to you. Prepackaged, sterilized "house plant soil" can be bought in variety stores and at garden centers. This is pretty poor stuff compared with the mediums we recommend.

Plants grown in many nurseries, and especially those coming from Florida, are potted in just about anything. The good heat, sun and humidity in greenhouses and the subtropics encourage rapid growth. But, once moved into the home, this soil becomes a liability. It is usually not sterilized into the bargain. *Get rid of it.*

If the plant you have bought at a florist's, nursery or garden center is potted in ordinary soil or sand (including cacti and succulents in the bricklike material usual in commercial dish gardens) give it a chance to recover from the change of environment for at least two weeks. Then knock the plant out of its pot, wash off all the soil you can in lukewarm water (very gently) and repot in one of the suitable house plant mixes we recommend. Follow directions in the section on repotting (page 20).

THE SOILLESS MIXES The so-called soilless mixes are made principally of peat moss, perlite and vermiculite. The combination produces a soil which is sterile, light in weight, well aerated and water-retentive. The components can be bought everywhere in small packages and stored easily in the house. They are clean and easy to handle. It is not necessary to make up a bushel of mix at a time. Formulas can be changed at will. And, most important, these mixes are far more effective in growing and blooming house plants than gardens or packaged soil. There are exceptions, of course, and we will mention them in their proper places. But, by and large, soilless mixes are a boon to the house plant grower.

Packaged Mixes. There *are* good packaged *soilless* mixes on the market. However most are too fine-grained and require the addition of some perlite. Read the label, which should list peat moss, perlite, vermiculite and a *minimum* of anything else. Some mixes contain fertilizer materials which limit their usefulness because they do not agree with all house plants.

Peat Moss. Sphagnum peat moss is natural, partly decomposed sphagnum moss (see details below). There are some peats which are made of sedge; always look for the sphagnum label. This is a fibrous brown material, fluffy when dry, which retains water and takes the place in our mix of humus and leaf molds. The nutritive value is low and it is somewhat acid; hence we add lime for those plants which are neutral, to offset this tendency. It is available in small bags, 1.7 cubic foot jiffy bales and large nursery-size bales. We prefer Canadian or German peat to Michigan peat.

Perlite. These snow-white feather light granules are produced by subjecting obsidian to intense heat. They take the place of coarse, gritty sand in our mixture and aerate it. Available in small and half-bushel bags.

Vermiculite. This is mica which has been exfoliated under intense heat. In other words, the extremely thin crystal platelets, which are compressed in nature, are separated. The result, in good-grade material, is a sort of cube with an accordion structure. Without any actual water absorption the crystals supply an enormous surface area to which water adheres by tension. The result is that vermiculite acts as a sponge without becoming soggy. It also fills in between the harder roundish granules of perlite. It is available in small and half-bushel bags.

Mica is a mined material which is very common and of many different grades. Some which is labeled "horticultural grade" is nothing of the sort in our opinion. The material is not exfoliated properly, is greasy to the touch and consists of rather flat, large particles, much like the inferior vermiculite used for insulation in the building trades. Look for those clean, accordionlike cubes.

Sphagnum Moss.   The moss itself, although not a component of our regular house plant mixes, is of considerable value in indoor growing. The live moss can be collected in bogs where it grows in immense quantities. Kept moist in a bag it will revive rapidly in a terrarium and is an ideal home for carnivorous plants. Dried, the whole plant serves as a mulch on the top of pots to keep roots cool and as a medium for some epiphytic (plants that grow on trees) tropical plants. The live moss will die if fertilized or subjected to impure water. The dead material can be fertilized like any soil.

Milled sphagnum moss is a medium used for seeding and vegetative propagation, and also as a substitute for peat moss in mixes. It has the capacity of preventing the development of the fungi which produce damp-off (a fungal disease) in young seedlings. For this reason it is highly recommended by some commercial seedsmen. Milled moss is available commercially in plastic bags.

The sphagnum plant has leaves which contain a number of empty cells for the purpose of water storage. The result is that it can absorb about twenty times its weight in water. When sphagnum is packed lightly into a pot, evaporation is rapid, with cooling effect very helpful on hot summer days when plants are likely to suffer.

Sand.   Although perlite is an excellent substitute, sand does the same job and deserves mention. With the exception of cacti and succulents, it is too heavy for most house plants and dries out much too rapidly. An additional reason why we use perlite is the difficulty of finding or buying good horticultural sand. It should not contain dust and *should* be very gritty. Nobody, to our knowledge, markets a superior sand for horticultural purposes in this country.

The pH Factor.   All plants are choosy about the degree of alkalinity or acidity in the soil. *Azalea* and *Ixora* are examples of plants which require very acid conditions. But most of our house plants prefer a nearly neutral soil. The scale used to determine the degree of acidity or alkalinity is called pH, and neutral is seven to eight on the scale, with lower numbers representing increasing acidity and higher numbers increasing alkalinity. pH has a good deal to do with a plant's ability to absorb and use fertilizer elements essential to plant growth.

If you are troubled by doubts about the acidity or alkalinity of the soil you are using, a simple test can be made with litmus paper. Tropical fish stores sell this in rolls with directions and a color chart for comparison. It is a very crude test but quite adequate for the average amateur indoor grower. To make more extensive and accurate tests you will need a soil-test kit such as can be bought through house plant-supply mail-order houses, which are listed on page 212.

Lime for Soilless Mixes. For those house plants requiring rather neutral soil, our peat moss is too low, in other words, too acid on the pH scale. In addition, the continuous action of watering increases acidity in the soil with time. For this reason we must use some lime in our mixes, as calcium alkalinizes the soil and raises the pH.

Lime comes as powdery horticultural lime, as limestone chips and as eggshell, which you can grind in a mortar and pestle or spin in the blender. It can be mixed in with the three other components of our soils. Powdered limestone goes into solution more quickly than the others. Therefore, in any of our formulas, use 1½ times as much eggshell or twice as much limestone chips by volume.

Ammonium Sulphate vs. Limey Water. In some parts of the country water contains a measurable quantity of lime. In that case, do not add lime to your mixes. On the contrary, your acid-loving plants may need treatment with ammonium sulfate to combat the calcium. Your county agricultural agent or local university can supply information on the amounts you will have to use diluted in each gallon of water when moistening your plants.

Water purifiers sometimes produce a liquid harmful to plants. Check with the manufacturer of the equipment before using purified water in your indoor garden.

HOMEMADE MIXES We give arbitrary names to the three mixes most commonly used in this book. They are not perfect for all the plants described; and, with experience, you may go in for refinements. But they will do a good job and are relatively foolproof.

Rich Mix.
By volume of dry material:
- 3 parts sphagnum peat moss
- 2 parts perlite
- 1 part vermiculite

Light Mix.
This is the so-called 1–1–1 mix or original Cornell Mix. By volume of dry material:
- 1 part sphagnum peat moss
- 1 part perlite
- 1 part vermiculite

Cactus–Succulent Mix.
By volume of dry material:
- 1 part sphagnum peat moss
- 2 parts perlite
- 2 parts vermiculite or sand

Adding Lime.
Where the need for lime is indicated in our text, these are the additions which you must make to the above formulas:

Rich Mix—5 level tablespoons powdered lime to a quart of mix.
Light Mix—3½ tablespoons powdered lime to a quart of mix.
Cactus–Succulent Mix—2 tablespoons powdered lime to a quart of mix.

POTS AND POTTING *Pots.* For most indoor growing of flowering exotics, plastic pots are more efficient than clay. Clay pots are heavy, take up more space and soil dries out much more rapidly than in plastics. However, since plastic pots are so light, tall plants leaning one way can tip them over. Invest in some lead sinkers—the kind that are used in salt-water fishing, available in sporting-goods stores. One or two three-ounce leads laid on top will stabilize a pot. If you have objections to plastic for esthetic reasons, you can find all kinds of decorative ceramic and lacquer pots on the market into which your plastic pot can be set and hidden from sight.

Unless you have ample room, keep your pots as small as possible in relation to the plants. A bit of potbinding does no harm except to a few plants which we mention in their cultural text. A supply of one-and-a-half-inch pots (the diameter rim to rim) for cuttings and young plants and a smaller number of two-and-a-half- and four-inch pots is usually sufficient for your needs. Larger sizes for the shrubbier plants can be bought individually. Square pots pack more closely than rounds.

Potting. For bare-rooted plants, use pots just large enough to accommodate them comfortably. Pour in a layer of mix, set the plant at the right height—the meeting of stem or leaf with root slightly below the outward curve of the rim; spread the roots and fill in soil gently. With a blunt tool—a flat stick, the handle of a spoon—press the soil inward from the inside edge of the pot toward the plant and continue to add soil until the level reaches the rim curve.

The reason for this procedure is to avoid downward pressure on the roots, which may damage them. Also, unless this is done, soil may not be packed against the side walls of the pot, with the result that, when the plant is watered, it will run down the crack and out of the pot without moistening the rest of the soil. Using soilless mixes, check your pot after a few weeks by poking a finger down in the corners. You may well find that the soil gives way, indicating open spaces below. Add soil so that the packing is even throughout the pot.

When moving a plant from a smaller to a larger pot, first knock it out gently so that the packed earth is not shaken loose around the roots. Watering an hour before you repot is helpful. If the new pot is taller than the old, pour some mix in the bottom, then set your plant in the middle. Be careful to push new soil all around the side walls with a blunt instrument so that no air holes remain.

With few exceptions, drainage in the pot is unnecessary. Since the plant and its pot will sit on a bed of pebbles or plastic crate (see below) the original purpose, to allow some aeration through the holes in the pot, is no longer valid. Drainage material just means that you need bigger pots and that there is less room for the roots to grow.

Most tropical herbaceous plants like rather loose potting. Shrubby, woody plants prefer a more compacted soil. Either way, water should sink through the medium rapidly. Still water on top indicates that you have packed the soil too hard or that the plant is potbound. If bubbles appear on the surface when you water the pot from the top, it is an indication that there is an air hole below. Poke the area and fill in with fresh soil.

FERTILIZER   Three elements are vital to all plant growth: nitrogen, phosphorus and potassium. On *all* labels of chemical or organic fertilizers the formula is always given in this order. The first number, therefore, indicates a nitrate, the second a phosphate and the third potash. The numbers indicate the degree of concentration. A 20–20–20 formula is twice as concentrated as a 10–10–10 formula. Labels on chemical and organic fertilizers indicate the manufacturer's idea of the amount to be diluted with a quart or a gallon of water.

All plants need feeding, but by and large we feed our house plants excessively. When using these formulas never use a concentration more than one fourth that recommended on the label. If the label says 1 teaspoon to a gallon, use only one quarter teaspoon.

The simplest and most practical rules to follow are:

1. For general growth of acid-loving plants use a formula high in nitrates—for instance, 30–10–10.

2. For general growth of other house plants use a balanced formula such as 20–20–20 or 10–10–10.

3. For encouraging bloom when the plant is mature choose a formula low in nitrates and high in the two other elements—for instance, 10–30–20 or 0–14–15.

Plants also need trace elements such as iron, molybdenum and boron. Buy chemical fertilizers that list such trace elements on their labels. Most organic fertilizers (fish emulsions, etc.) contain them. There is no evidence that organics are "better" than chemical fertilizers.

Acid plants suffer occasionally from iron deficiency. This can be remedied by using Sequestrene (Ge   llowing directions on the package. Yellowing and dr   the sign of this condition, but check first whethe   done by insects.

How Often to Fer   f two methods. The
best   e fourth the strength
                            other is to fertilize
                            nth to one fifteenth
                            be equivalent to a
                            ants.
                            hout any fertilizer
                            oil is to encourage
                            ou want to keep
                            er than we have

                            ly stops growing
                            er absorbing the
                            ng program will
                            ay be due to any
                            Do not fertilize
                            loom starts. An
                            nable to utilize

Leaching.   No plant ever absorbs *all* the fertilizer you give it. So there is a constant buildup of superfluous salts in the soil. This must be eliminated periodically. The best procedure is to water plants thoroughly once a month and allow the pots to drain, thus carrying away the salts.

WATERING   We have indicated the amount of watering required by each plant in the text of the plant descriptions. At best these are only approximations, and you will have to learn by practice and experience. We have no preferences regarding watering from top or bottom. And we know a number of house plants which, contrary to the warnings of the experts, are quite happy sitting in a saucer of water most of the time.

Most plant losses do come from over- or underwatering. The over-watering occurs with those which prefer just-moist conditions—less often with ones which prefer to be rather dry. Underwatering may be a matter of just one day of neglect, which can be quite sufficient to kill a plant. This does not mean that you need to water every day. It does mean that you must examine every plant every day and decide whether it should be watered or not.

We prefer to draw water lukewarm from the hot-water faucet than from the cold one. The former usually contains less chemicals needing aeration. The water should always be at least room temperature.

Water more during active growth. When plants stop growing, reduce watering. Water more during warm spells than cold spells. Never pour cold water on the leaves.

The speed with which moisture dries out in the soil of your pots depends on the amount of soil relative to the size of the plant, the packing of the soil and absorption by the plant. That is why you cannot count on all your plants needing water at the same time. It is most interesting to observe the difference in plants in respect to the amount of water they absorb. There are some which are forever thirsty and others, which may be much larger, which use up very little water. In summer it is not at all unusual to find the soil in the pot of a thirsty plant bone dry in the evening after you have watered thoroughly in the morning. These plants are also the first to succumb if they are com-pletely deprived of moisture in the soil for even a few hours. Our tropical blooming plants are often particularly sensitive on this point and will suffer if neglected.

Spraying and Misting. We are careful in our use of these two words throughout this book. Spraying can mean setting a plant under a bath-room shower and thoroughly dousing it. Or it can mean the showering of a plant with a spray can which completely covers the leaves with water—so that they drip.

Misting requires a very fine nozzle for the spray. The moisture is deposited on the plant in such fine droplets that they do not coagulate and run off the leaves.

The effect of spray is much like rain. The effect of misting is to increase greatly the humidity on the surface of leaves—much like the conditions in a cloud forest.

Some plants—orchids in particular—will develop fungus diseases if sprayed but benefit greatly from misting.

Always remember this essential difference when you spray or mist.

While on Vacation. Plants can be kept happy for several weeks while you are away from home by means of wicks. These are lengths of fiber glass which are poked in through the bottoms of the pots well into the soil and which dangle into a tray containing water. Many growers do all their watering in this way. They are just as effective and a lot cheaper than special wick pots or tubes provided with moisture sensors. Most house plant supply houses carry the wicking material.

A new type of wick called "Water Wick" works from the outside of the pot, reaching from a container of water into the top surface of the soil. A number of gadgets on the market provide a container for water and a tube with a ceramic sensor at the end. The sensor is forced into the soil and releases water whenever the medium dries out.

TEMPERATURE   Most of us live in warm homes, therefore the best plants for us are those which share our preference. Our own choice of plants takes this into consideration. However, a few requiring cool temperatures are also listed. We don't grow them ourselves because we are with the warm majority. But, then, we live and grow in an apartment. Growers living in houses can sometimes enjoy the best of both worlds and have one place for warmth-loving plants and another for plants that like it cool.

The warmth-loving plants must have a day temperature throughout the year of sixty-five degrees minimum in order to bloom. And very few will do so if the temperature drops below sixty degrees at night when they are setting buds. A drop of ten degrees from day to night temperatures is beneficial, but it must start at higher levels—seventy-five day to sixty-five night for instance.

The heat of August in un-air-conditioned rooms seems to be lethal to some plants. We still don't know exactly why, or what to do about it. This is perhaps the time when fans become vital pieces of equipment.

Provide air motion in August by all means. Once your plants are past that month, their health intact, the rest of the year will present no temperature problems in an average home.

Air conditioning has the advantages of preserving fairly even temperatures, especially not excessively high ones, and of providing some air motion. But it does lower humidity. Provide that essential by means of a humidifier and you will have a superior environment for plant bloom.

HUMIDITY   Our own plants, with few exceptions, are tropical in origin and are accustomed to high humidity. Fifty percent relative humidity or higher encourages growth and bloom. In winter humidity in the average home often is well below thirty percent. You will have to do something about this if you want continuous bloom.

A simple way to provide humidity in a partially enclosed space—a shelf or cabinet, for instance—is to have your trays partially filled with pebbles and a water level just below their surfaces. The water should not touch the bottoms of the pots. Plastic crate is even better for the purpose as it is lighter and cleaner. About three-quarters of an inch thick, it is a waffle-design diffuser often used in elevators under the fluorescent lamps. You can get it from plastics supply stores in two foot by four foot sheets, which you can saw to proper size. It makes a much handsomer support for your pots.

VENTILATION   Experience with terrarium and bottle gardening supplies sufficient proof that even flowering plants are not altogether dependent on moving or "fresh" air. Opening windows in the city apartment does more harm than good since it lets in soot and smog. In the country it makes no noticeable difference. We keep air moving by means of fans or open windows principally for one purpose—to keep heat from building up in the plant area either from the sun's rays or the fluorescent tubes.

In cities and their suburbs aerial pollution is a real menace to plants and a common, not easily recognized, cause of failure. Certain plants, Achimenes and some orchids for instance, are especially sensitive and just will not bloom in an atmosphere loaded with chemicals.

TRIMMING AND PRUNING An important part of the culture of any plant in the house which has a branching or vining habit is pruning and trimming to keep it within the space allotted to it and improve appearance and vigor. If we want to keep a plant which is a rapid grower from constantly needing bigger pots, we will have to prune it rather drastically. There is a point which some reach when the growth of branches exhausts the ability of the roots confined in the pot to supply sufficient nourishment. What follows is a kind of strangulation which causes leaf drop and can be lethal. We then have the alternative of transplanting to larger quarters or, what is often more convenient, cutting the plant back so that the roots can support it.

Certain plants tend to develop long spindly branches in the early stages of growth. They are really begging for a good trim, which will strengthen and thicken the base of each branch so it is able to support further branching and growth. Neglect spindly branches and they will just continue to stretch, becoming progressively weaker and more unsightly, without any corresponding development of strength to support the additional greenery.

For newcomers to house plants, this business of ruthlessly cutting branches is often a traumatic experience. People become attached to plants as they do to pets and feel that they are torturing them when they apply the scissors. On the contrary, the growth is presumed to be involuntary, like hair on a dog, and we are doing the plant a kindness when we prune it back to respectable size and health.

Trimming can be an art—as in bonsaiing plants. Bonsai is not a subject in which we are specialists, and there are other books describing the quite complicated processes in great detail. But for the ordinary needs of your plants, there is no need for such refinements.

The general principle of pruning for health and appearance is altogether simple and can be summed up in a single sentence: Any plant whose branches are weak or are spreading in an unattractive way should be cut back to the shape desired. Remove the end of each branch by making a cut just above a node or leaf base. Stems between nodes are leafless and the bare tips spoil the appearance of the plant. It is common practice to prune even more than is immediately necessary, as the plant is growing all the time and will fill out rapidly. Do not hesitate to remove branches with buds or flowers, as more vigorous bloom will be encouraged by your surgery.

In the early stages of the growth of a seedling or cutting, even plants with a naturally bushy habit often put up single stems which will not branch in the house unless induced to do so. When the plant is of a height where you would like to see the branching start for best appearance, simply remove the two to four leaves at the tip. Lateral branching usually starts immediately.

Light

WINDOWSILL AND SUN PORCH The biggest problem blooming plants indoors has always been providing them with enough light. We have to consider the length of time the sun shines through the window each day and also its intensity. Because of smog, city-grown plants receive about thirty percent less light than in the country. Therefore almost all indoor plants bloom better in the country than in the city.

A sun porch receives about half the light of a greenhouse. Walls and ceilings cut down the period of direct sunlight drastically. Because of the ceiling, the plants can only receive angled light in the early morning and late afternoon when it is less intense. In winter there are longer hours of direct sunlight than in summer (because the sun is lower in the sky), usually offset by a greater number of clouded days.

The windowsill is even more restricted because the space is smaller. Only the plants directly in the center and close to the sill receive direct light for several hours on a sunny day. Every inch to the side or rear cuts down the duration of sunlight to a measurable extent.

While great progress has been made with the introduction of plants which will bloom under these light conditions, do not count on year-round bloom—for that you must have supplementary artificial light, discussed in the next section.

All the plants listed will grow and bloom on a windowsill in the city with a south or west exposure. The east in the city is rarely suitable for blooming. Remember, however, that exposure is not everything. A window or sun porch in the country which is heavily shaded by vines or trees is no better than a city window. A south window in the city blocked from the sun by a tall building does not qualify as a good growing space. Dirty windows don't help. The proximity of radiators or leaky window frames may make a seemingly favorable exposure quite impossible.

Because of inferior light conditions in the city, plants which in the country do best in reflected light must be set in full sunlight in an apartment window. The African Violet is a good example. But this does not solve the problem completely because the sun's heat can be as damaging as the rays are beneficial. There is no sure and simple way of specifying the amount of natural light required by these indoor plants simply because of the infinite number of different situations and the unpredictable behavior of some of our new tropical plants. Even old garden favorites react differently indoors than we would expect—those requiring full sunlight outdoors doing very well on a bright windowsill and others with lower requirements in the garden demanding the best light we can provide.

In this book, full sun means five hours of direct sunlight, partial sun two hours. Bright reflected light calls for some direct sun but less than two hours. Reflected or indirect light is a position protected from the direct rays of the sun but with five hours of real brightness.

Among our plants are a few that require long nights and short days to initiate bloom. For them seasonal changes in day length in a window are an advantage. However, they are dependent on complete darkness during the night period, and light from your living area or from a street lamp is sufficient to prevent bloom.

GROWING UNDER ARTIFICIAL LIGHT   Artificial light gardening is an entirely new kind of horticulture which has already produced phenomenal results. This has occurred in spite of the fact that the light source is far less intense than the sun. The reason is twofold. The number of light hours can be extended, and there are no cloudy days.

To this must be added the beneficial effects of a light which does not change in intensity and an environment which varies little with the seasons. Readers who seek details on the method should read *The Indoor Light Gardening Book* (Crown).

Supplemental Light.   With supplemental artificial light, house plants can be bloomed in city windows all the year. In the country it is needed more as a substitute light source on cloudy days, especially in winter, than as a constant boost for insufficient light on sunny days.

Depending on the width of window, suspend a two-tube twenty-four-inch, forty-eight-inch or ninety-six-inch fluorescent fixture with reflector over the plants and provide light on dark days or supplemental light after sundown—or both. Electrical-equipment stores supply sensors which will turn on the lights automatically whenever outdoor light approaches darkness and switch them off as the sun comes out. A timer limits the day length, so that the lights will be off for a predetermined period. The darkness should be of eight or nine hours' duration. This allows for a supplemental artificially lighted period of from three to seven hours, not including stretches of lighting during cloudy days.

Use one Warm White to one Cool White or Daylight tube for best results. We consider the best *single* tube for blooming to be Gro-Lux Wide Spectrum. The fixture should not be more than fifteen or eighteen inches higher than the blooming tops of the plants. Farther away they will still be beneficial but not nearly so effective.

THE INDOOR LIGHT GARDEN   A true light garden depends entirely on artificial light. Its great advantage is that it can be located anywhere in the house or apartment. By itself it is far more dependable than a windowsill for blooming plants.

The minimum efficient fixture is two twenty-watt fluorescent tubes with reflector, twenty-four inches long. Forty-watt, forty-eight-inch and seventy-two-watt, ninety-six-inch lamps are still more effective. The fixture can be hung from or attached to any plane surface—ceiling or shelf. The reflector can be dispensed with when the surface to which the fixture is attached is painted flat white.

For a light garden a few other things are required—a timer, trays, drainage or support material in the trays, pots, and, of course, plants. It can be strictly utilitarian or part of the furniture of a living area. You can adapt simple metal or wood shelving to suit your needs. Cabinets are ideal for the purpose.

Light gardening has advanced to the point that, with special equipment, it is possible to bloom any kind of flowering plant. However, in listing plants that really bloom, we are mindful of the needs and limitations of the average home grower. The unit considered here as our standard of measurement is a two-tube fluorescent fixture with reflector. The tubes are forty watts and forty-eight inches long. One is a Cool White or Daylight tube and the other a Warm White. Such a unit is available with a stand so that it can be placed on a table. Any plant we describe can be bloomed with this unit.

Our preference for the Warm White and Daylight or Cool White commercial tubes in combination is based on information gathered from light gardeners, noncommercial experts, and our own experience. Of the so-called "growth" lamps we consider the Gro-Lux Wide Spectrum to be the best. This is not the same as the Gro-Lux tube, which is more expensive. Incandescent bulbs add little to the efficiency of fluorescent fixtures in the light garden. Standard spot and flood lamps—especially the G.E. Cool Beam—are useful for maintaining foliage plants but are ineffective for blooming plants. High output fluorescent tubes, for which there was a short vogue, offer no advantage, cost more and use more electricity. The enormously powerful vapor lamps (Metalarc, Metal Halide, Lucalox, etc.) are not yet adapted to home use.

There is a considerable gain when more than two tubes are rowed up next to each other. There is some disagreement about how far apart these tubes should be. A distance of four to six inches between centers seems about right. As more tubes are added it is possible to move plants farther from the lights than we have indicated as necessary for a two-tube fixture. When an entire ceiling is covered with fluorescent tubes, plants at floor level in the center receive almost as much light as they do within a foot of the tubes. This means that quite large plants can be grown and bloomed. Of course, such installations are expensive, and not many have tried them. Our two-tube fixture does a good job and is not costly.

Once you have tried light gardening, you will not give up your windowsill garden, for it has its uses. But you will find the former far more successful in blooming plants indoors.

Standard practice is to leave the lights on for fourteen to sixteen hours a day. According to the growth habits of the flowering plant, it should be within a distance of fifteen inches from two-tube fixtures. Very often bloom can be achieved only when the top of the plant almost touches the lights. The distance plants must be set in relation to the lamps also depends on the other factors in the environment and on your cultural methods. There are no absolute rules to go by. In an outdoors garden, too, it is often necessary to move plants around until a place is found where they will grow well. In the same way you must experiment with the behavior of your plants under lights. In plant descriptions we do give suggestions on the best position.

The lamps must be changed about once a year as they are constantly declining in intensity during use. Long tubes are more efficient than short ones because about three inches at either end of a tube of any length give out very little light. Standard lengths are twenty-four inches, forty-eight inches, seventy-two inches and ninety-six inches. Normally a forty-eight-inch tube costs no more than a twenty-four-incher.

Larger light gardens (those with more than two tubes) are more efficient. Tiered stands give more space. Deep shelves allow for the placement of more tubes so that a greater amount of light reaches the plants.

FLOWERING TERRARIUMS Old-fashioned terrariums contain plantings of woodland greenery perpetuating in the house in winter a remembrance of the summer season. The modern flowering terrarium serves an entirely different purpose, being a year-round decorative feature of the home. It requires very little care, and certain plants are happier in the environment than anywhere else. Wherever there are pets (cats) the containers are a safe refuge for the plants.

Terrariums come in all shapes and sizes. Among the most inexpensive are tropical fish tanks; these are also an ideal shape for landscaping miniature gardens. Brandy snifters, glass laboratory tanks, and vases are among the many choices. There are also numerous plastic models on the market. Some are well designed, but they suffer, compared with glass, from the fact that all plastic materials sooner or later are eroded or scratched by the soil used in them.

A terrarium is any transparent vessel with cover for growing plants; the opening may be large or small. Bottle gardens are merely a form of terrarium with a very narrow opening requiring long narrow tools for planting. But whether the opening is narrow or wide, the principle of terrarium operation is that the garden is largely self-sustaining due to the fact that the opening is kept closed most of the time.

A terrarium functions best when the moisture in the soil is just about enough to sustain life. This means that it is not wet, but rather just moist to the touch. When the terrarium is sealed, moisture evaporates from the plants and the soil, creating stable high humidity. The plants recycle the air in the container. Thus, ideally, a terrarium should never need attention, and indeed, perfectly healthy ones have been maintained for ten years and more without being opened once.

There are a number of reasons why we no longer keep terrariums closed all the time. Since ours are intended to be decorative, we cannot let the plants within grow wild. Whether we use flowering or foliage material, we have to keep them neat. To bloom plants we need more light than was required to maintain plants from the woodland floor which grow in continuous shade. Light also means heat. Whether because of a fluorescent tube or the sunlight in a window, there are times when the interior of the terrarium becomes overheated and we are obliged to leave it partly open. In the old-fashioned terrarium gardens, the plants were set right in the soil. If they grew too big or were not doing well, removing them destroyed the whole planting as all the roots became mingled in the process of growing. For this reason we use small plastic pots (maximum four inches in diameter) for all our terrarium plants, burying them in the soil so that they are not visible. If we have to make a change they are easily removed and replaced.

The use of pots is quite new and is far more practical than the old methods. We cannot expect a decorative growing terrarium garden to remain static or last forever. Some foliage plants are slow-growing, but most of them are not, and the flowering plants are even less so. To keep a terrarium garden going for a year without change is something of a challenge. In most instances we do have to change plants and pots from time to time. A very few can be set right in the soil without risk. The best of these are *Sinningia pusilla* and *concinna,* which have very small roots and will seed themselves, producing new plants around them with little risk of overcrowding. Most of the standard foliage plants recommended in the brochures accompanying terrarium kits will fill up the container in next to no time.

Potted plants in a terrarium cannot spread their roots throughout the medium and adjust the extent of this growth according to their individual needs. So plants in pots do dry out, since they are unable to draw on the total moisture in the foundation soil of the garden. This means more watering, with a frequency which depends on the habit of the plant. It will always be less often than for a plant growing outside a terrarium, but once every two weeks is common.

Terrarium gardens may take many different forms. Sometimes the container is only used as a frame and a protection. No soil is used, and the plants placed inside are exposed pots. The floor of the terrarium—usually a tank—is simply covered with pebbles. and the two, three or four potted plants are placed on them. If the plants are well chosen the effect is most decorative, while growth is excellent due to the even high humidity and temperature.

Most terrarium gardens do contain soilless mix. At the bottom, beginners should lay a base of drainage material—perlite, limestone chips or charcoal—one eighth the height of the total soil. The minimum height of the soil is estimated according to the size of the pots you will be using—so that they can be buried. But it should not be less than one and a half inches. With greater experience you can eliminate drainage completely. It is suggested only because of the risk that the novice will overwater the mix and that there will be excess draining out of the medium. Without drainage the terrarium looks and functions better.

The remaining medium should consist of soilless mix containing equal quantities by volume of Canadian peat moss, perlite and vermiculite, with additional lime. Calculate two tablespoons of horticultural lime to eight cups of mix. Lime is unnecessary if you use lime chips for drainage.

Add two cups of water to eight cups of dry mix and you will have just the right amount of moisture.

Start putting the mix into the tank over the drainage material, building up a scene with stones for accent and as support in places where the mix is likely to slip. If you leave part of the drainage uncovered and build up from there in other areas of the terrarium you will get an effect of greater height. Set in your pots with plants wherever they will look best, tilting the ones on the sides of the terrarium toward the center of the scene. Pack soil around them so that they are hidden. Additional stones will help do this and at the same time add to the visual effect. When everything has been planted, lay a paving of decorative stones. With a narrow-spouted watering can, pour a gentle stream down the inside of the glass of the container, cleaning it and at the same time providing just enough water to moisten the drainage itself. If there is any excess water in the drainage, the cover of the terrarium must be left off for several days until it has all disappeared.

Provided that your mix is just moist and not wet, you can now put a glass cover on the opening of your container. No fertilizer at all is needed as, with proper lighting, the conditions are ideal and the small amount of nutrition in the peat mix in your pot is sufficient. It may be a good idea, however, to water once every six months with a little 20–20–20 balanced fertilizer in solution. Remember, you do not want your plants to grow rapidly. They will bloom without fertilizer.

If you have an air-conditioned room for the terrarium, or if temperatures remain in the sixty-five–seventy-two degrees F. range, it may not be necessary to remove the covering of the terrarium for months on end unless the pots become dry. If the heat within builds up over eighty–eighty-five degrees F., move the cover partly aside for ventilation. With the cover partly open you must watch the moisture content of your terrarium more closely.

Many commercial terrariums and kits are sold these days without any hint that the plantings will need light. It is a widespread fallacy that they can be set anywhere in the home where they happen to provide a decorative feature. This is far from the truth. The failure of your terrarium is almost a certainty unless it has a favorable situation where it receives a considerable amount of light. The flowering terrarium requires as much light as any windowsill or fluorescent-lighted plant.

Terrariums can be maintained close to a windowsill. They will not tolerate direct sunlight because of the heat buildup within the container;

bright indirect light is sufficient. Basically, however, the window is not a good place for a terrarium. The principal reason is that the light is all from the outside and the plants naturally grow in that direction. From within a room what you will see is not at all what you may have planned. If you have built a landscape, the front of the container must face the window, and you see only the back. If the soil is not built up your plants will still be turned away from you.

With fluorescent light, which is set above the terrarium, the scene faces toward you and the plants grow straight and evenly.

The best fluorescent lights for terrariums are either a two-tube twenty-watt fixture using one Warm White and one Cool White tube or a Circline fluorescent fixture using one Warm White tube of twenty-two watts, eight and one quarter inches in diameter. The strip fixture is best for tanks or for small terrariums—snifters and such—in a row. Attach it under shelving, cabinets or tables. The Circline serves for large, round terrariums and is particularly suited for fitting into table lamps with large half-dome reflectors. You will need a timer to turn your lights on and off. Fourteen hours daily of light is sufficient for bloom.

Multiplying Your Plants

Reproducing plants is a most important, and enjoyable, aspect of indoor growing. It is the only way to ensure a constant supply of healthy, maturing plants and of preserving those which please us the most.

Plants we buy at the nursery suffer a severe shock moving to our homes. If it is too much for them, they will die off rather quickly. Therefore, we follow the invariable rule with any worthwhile plant, of immediately taking cuttings and starting new plants. As they are conditioned from the outset to the home environment, they usually do better than the nursery-grown plant.

Our favorites do not last forever and cannot easily be replaced from a nursery just when we want them. So it is advisable, before a plant has passed its prime, to take leaf or stem cuttings and start new plants which will be exactly like the old ones.

Not all flowering house plants can be multiplied by means of cuttings. The bulb plants are obvious exceptions. Others are a few of the annuals, though experience has shown that more of them are amenable to this method than had formerly been considered possible. Usually house plants which cannot be propagated by vegetative means have seeds which germinate quickly and are also fast growers.

There are numerous ways of carrying out vegetative and seed propagation, all of which have proved relatively satisfactory in practice.

Plant Problems

COMBATING INSECTS Don't get in a panic if you find insects on your plants. Don't immediately throw them out. In the house preventing and getting rid of damaging pests is fairly easy, and the methods we use will not expose you to poisonous fumes or harmful contact.

A number of the most troublesome insects are invisible to the naked eye. Everybody who raises plants should get a 10-power loupe, a little magnifying glass which can be purchased in hobby and optical shops, or a contact-print magnifier available in photography shops. Most people don't take this advice and prefer to suffer. The loupe is not an infernal machine, and you might just as well see what is wrong with your plant.

Nine times out of ten, if your plant develops blotchy leaves or they start dropping off, the cause is an infestation. Examine the tops and bottoms of leaves carefully with the magnifier. If you see fine webbings, collections of little transparent eggs and areas of leaf which are translucent, you have bugs, whether you see them or not. You may wonder how they got on the plant. The answer is that they fly in or are transported from anywhere and everywhere. You bring them into the house on your clothes; they fly in through the window or the front door. Every time you buy a plant you risk bringing in live insects or eggs which will hatch in a short time.

PESTICIDES WE USE   Because there are always new developments in the field of pesticides, our own methods have been changing. We now use the No-Pest Strip, Benlate or Benomyl, Black Leaf 40 and alcohol or chlorinated water almost exclusively. For the specific needs referred to below we may occasionally use Kelthane, VC-13 and malathion.

The No-Pest Strip is made by Shell Chemical Company. A piece of thick plastic six and one half inches long, it is impregnated with V*apona*® Insecticide which vaporizes at a controlled rate. The Strip is extremely effective in combating many types of plant pests when hung right in the midst of the indoor garden area. Pay careful attention to the warnings printed on the package regarding location of the Strip. Do not touch the No-Pest Strip with your bare hands. If you do not care to hang it in your home as a preventive, you can treat specific plants for insects by enclosing plant and pot in a plastic bag with a one-inch piece of the Strip for eight to twelve hours. A longer period may harm the plant; but the process can be repeated at intervals of two or three days until examination of the plant with a magnifier confirms the absence of insect life.

Benlate or Benomyl.   Benlate is a Dupont fungicide, which, with somewhat different dispersing agents, is packaged and distributed by others as Benomyl. You can buy Benomyl in small packages at plant-supply stores. Benlate sells by the pound and is expensive for the amateur.

It has recently been found that these fungicides are effective in destroying the fertility of mite eggs both when used in the soil as a systemic and when sprayed on the leaves and branches of a plant. This is an important breakthrough, as mite is our most persistent plant enemy. These fungicides are virtually harmless to human beings when used correctly. Follow instructions on the label.

VC-13. This is an effective soil insecticide. We usually dilute it in a pail of water and wear rubber gloves when dipping plants. It is not pleasant stuff and we prefer to avoid it. VC-13 is effective against nematodes, but if one of our plants has them, this is one instance when we prefer to throw it out rather than take any chance of these creatures spreading in our garden.

Malathion. Though it has a horrible odor, malathion is supposed to be relatively harmless. We use it only for mealybugs on cacti and succulents. Plant and pot should be dipped. However, never bring any member of the Crassula family in contact with malathion—the results are absolutely lethal.

Kelthane is effective against mites but has a powerful odor and must be used with every precaution. We use it occasionally as a dip but prefer the No-Pest Strip or Benomyl.

Black Leaf 40 is a nicotine sulphate insecticide effective against aphids.

House and Garden Raid. We hate to use sprays at all in the house. However a couple of blasts at a distance of four or five feet from a plant usually rid it of white fly.

Alcohol and Chlorinated Water. Rubbing alcohol and a brush help remove scale. A tablespoon of Clorox in a gallon of water is recommended for a variety of insects, but we cannot vouch for it.

COMMON PESTS   *Mealybugs.* White, fuzzy, oval and flat creatures which move quite slowly. There are many kinds, some of which are visible only as very tiny white dots. When mature they form a gooey mass which is similar to a cocoon. Don't think that because you have removed all the bugs in sight that you are really rid of them. Under the loupe you will see the next generation, unbelievably small, heading out to forage in all directions.

47

Cure. Have a No-Pest Strip hanging nearby or enclose the plant with a piece of it in a plastic bag for eight to twelve hours. Repeat a week later. Or dip the pot in VC-13. Dip cacti and succulents other than Crassulas in malathion. The dips will eliminate insects in the soil plus any which are in the saucer or crawling around the pot.

White Fly. A nuisance with Fuchsias and Lantanas, etc. They fly up when a plant is disturbed. The underparts of leaves usually harbor their visible eggs. The regenerative cycle is two or three days.

Cure. Hang a No-Pest Strip nearby. Spray the plant with House and Garden Raid.

Springtails. These little insects run around in the soil and start hopping when you water.

Cure. Dip pot in VC-13 solution.

Mites. There are all kinds of mites—short-legged spiderlike creatures visible only with a ten-power loupe. If there are delicate bits of white webbing on the backs of leaves you can be sure that you have mites, even if you cannot see a single one. They multiply rapidly and are very destructive. Very high humidity and frequent wettings keep them at bay. But the moment the air becomes dry, certain plants are attacked immediately. The No-Pest Strip hung in the garden area is a trouble-free means of protection.

Cure. Chase mites with water. A thorough drenching of a plant for a few days running will usually rid you of these pests. Spraying the plant or dipping it in a solution of Benlate or Benomyl is the new cure.

Aphids. Little green sucking insects, quite visible and multiplying rapidly.

Cure. Wash the plant off thoroughly in lukewarm water and spray with Black Leaf 40.

Nematodes. There are two types of these minute worms, those which live in the soil and others on the leaves. When you have soil nematodes your plant just droops and starts to die for no apparent reason. It may look very much like fungal rot at the base of the stem. In fact there is no definite indication of these pests. But if you unpot a plant, wash off its roots and find small nodules on them, you have nematodes. Get rid of the plant. There are nemacides which are effective—notably Kelthane —but this pest is so dangerous for your whole garden that you should take no chances.

Leaves attacked by nematodes look as if they had fungal disease. It is only when you use the loupe that you see the transparent, amazingly wiggly worms along the edges of the leaves. Dipping in Kelthane is a cure. But we don't fool around with this nematode. Usually we take a deep breath and discard the plant.

Scale. Scale are little brown, sometimes cream-colored, insects which lie flat against stem or leaf, especially along the mid-veins of the latter.

Cure. Take a stiffish brush and dip in rubbing alcohol. Then scrub the scale off, especially along the mid-veins of leaves. Hanging a No-Pest Strip nearby is both preventive and cure.

USING BUGS TO FIGHT BUGS

Praying mantis and ladybugs (or -birds) have been much recommended lately as house pets which will devour all your insects free of charge. This doesn't work in the house. In the first place, your garden does not normally have enough insects to feed a respectable ladybug, much less a praying mantis, in the manner to which it is accustomed. Ladybugs can't handle the bigger insects. Praying mantis usually end up by consuming each other down to the last lady. Mealybugs, mites, etc., are beneath their notice. As adults you might try putting them to work on your cockroaches.

Ladybugs will hatch and swarm through the house. In no time you will have them in bed, among your linens, and up the sleeves of your clothes hanging in the closet. You may have to take to flight long before they have rid your plants of insects. Better let her ladyship stay at home with her children and prevent fires.

COMBATING FUNGUS INFECTIONS

Plants are subject to innumerable fungal infections. Since fungus spores are always present in the air and soil, our plants would soon succumb to them if it were not that only a weakness in the plant itself or a special condition in the environment permits them to grow and multiply. These conditions are due to excessive watering, watering during cool spells, root burn due to excessive use of fertilizers, and extreme heat combined with high humidity.

Most fungal infections are impossible for the amateur to tell apart. The one called Botrytis appears as a definite rotting of the stem of a plant where it joins the roots. It is called crown rot in African Violets. Powdery mildew appears on smooth leaves as a gray film, followed by dropping of the leaves. But there are innumerable others which are usually visible as forms of localized rotting: black spots on leaves; areas of rot on stems.

In our experience as indoor gardeners we have had very little occasion to use fungicides at all, and we suspect that this is generally true of indoor growing because if a plant gets stem or crown rot, the situation is too far gone for any fungicide to be effective. Prevention is a matter of providing healthy conditions for the plant rather than of spraying constantly with fungicides.

The two fungicides with which we are most familiar are Fermate (or Ferbam) and Benlate (or Benomyl). We use Fermate on the wounded parts of plants, which are subject to infection. If a tuber is partly rotted, we cut out the infected section down to healthy tissue and dust with Fermate. We have used Benlate as a spray on black spot of rose leaves and on certain Begonias (the Rieger Begonias, for instance) which are very subject to mildew.

A special form of infection which attacks young seedlings is called damp-off. You can't stop it but you can prevent it. We have never had trouble with damp-off. First of all, we use only sterilized soilless mix. Secondly, the use of a thin coating of milled sphagnum moss has anti-fungal action on the seedlings. Follow this method for planting seeds and you will have no trouble.

The one plant family which, more than any other, is subject to these diseases, even when the environment appears to be favorable, are the orchids. Benlate has recently been widely used, replacing other, older products. However, the reader should consult specialized orchid literature on this subject, since the situation is constantly changing.

Buying Flowering House Plants

When you buy a gift plant at a nursery or florist shop you naturally choose one which is fully mature and is blooming well. A particularly fine plant is an evidence of friendship and generosity. You judge not by the basic excellence of the plant for growing in the house but rather for sheer spectacular appearance. Most gift plants will be thrown out when they have finished blooming, and you as well as the recipient are happy if they have provided a few weeks of pleasure.

Choosing the house plants you expect to live with is another matter. You should know that a pot of Chrysanthemums, an Azalea bush or large Cyclamens and Calceolarias are not candidates for a longevity record. Plants of this kind have been most popular in the past because the idea of maintaining blooming plants in the house did not occur to anyone. That is changing now as more and more people become aware that this is practical. Hopefully the good plants which now can only be bought in special nurseries will find a larger market and start turning up at regular florist shops and garden centers.

The first consideration in buying plants for home maintenance and bloom is that one's choice possesses the necessary qualities to exist in the new environment. Our descriptive list of plants is meant to be a guide to the selection of such plants.

Secondly, we would be defeating the whole purpose of our new interest in blooming plants indoors if we bought only fully mature ones in full flower. This is a mistake that so many people still make who have had enough experience to know better. The attraction of a plant that looks pretty is irresistible. But a fully mature blooming plant in its prime —one that has been on the upgrade ever since it was started from seed or cutting—will most probably be on the downgrade from the moment you bring it home. The very shock of the change in environment will accelerate the aging process.

One thing must be made clear, though this should not be necessary: plants do not last forever. Like everything else they have their youth, maturity and old age. We have known quite experienced plant growers to ask why some favorite is no longer blooming or growing. Quite often the cause is simply old age. The stems and branches have become woody and sections of root no longer function. What is needed is a new generation—which is why we continually propagate our plants.

The upshot of all this is that we should buy young house plants— ones that are well rooted and shapely, possibly in bud, but not necessarily (for the change shock may blast the buds). If you know what kind of plant you are buying and how it will flower, if you know that it has the right characteristics to perform well in the house, then your small, unflowered plant is the best buy. Now you can bring it home with the assurance that it will suffer less from the trip and that it will be increasing in size for a long time—that when flowers appear they are the first of a long series, not the end of one. You can shape the young plant to your own taste, and it will have much more time to acclimate itself to your home.

SIZE AND SCALE IN HOUSE PLANTS

One of the hardest adjustments we must make to blooming house plants is becoming accustomed to the relatively small size of many of the flowers. Some of these plants would be lost in a garden, where the scale is related to the great outdoors, to trees and to houses. Plants and flowers must be massed or be individually very large to compete with these massive objects. Also, when we are in a garden we look down on plants or across at them. The tall ones are at eye level and the small ones form a carpet in which we do not perceive much detail.

In a greenhouse, the size of the building and the great quantities of plants has a similar effect. Their size is not quite so important, but it still makes the difference between a plant which is visible at first sight or one which is lost in the multitude.

The scale of our living rooms is much smaller still. Walls are a neutral background broken by shelving or pictures. Most of our *objets d'art* are modest in size. In such an environment foliage plants can be quite big as they are a sort of green furniture and are in proportion to chairs and sofas. You will notice, however, that we instinctively pick smaller foliage plants for the house than for the reception room of an office or for a bank.

Dahlias are examples of flowers which are grown outdoors to a huge size. They look just fine on their tall leafy plants. Bring them into the house and they are overwhelming and gross. The whole scale of things indoors is more intimate. We see them at a distance of inches or a few feet, not of yards. So our smaller plants look in perfect proportion, and the very little ones, like *Sinningia pusilla*, which would be altogether too small in a garden or greenhouse, look charming and have personality in a terrarium or a brandy snifter on the sideboard.

Don't, therefore, make the mistake of buying the big plants at a nursery. Acquire small and attractive ones, and more of them. Properly displayed in the house, plants that are no more than a few inches tall and whose flowers may be much less than an inch in size, will make a perfectly adequate, often spectacular, show.

There is one other point. We do not treat garden plants as individuals. We almost invariably do so indoors. Each plant is a world to itself and an element of importance in our room decoration. We do not mass house plants; we see and live with each one much as we do with our animal pets.

Plants Grouped by Special Characteristics: Twelve Lists

All reference to plants listed refers to those plants specifically mentioned in the Cultural Section which follows.

1. EASE OF BLOOM IN THE HOUSE

All our plants are *relatively* easy to grow and bloom. Nevertheless, some are, of course, easier than others. We can rate them as Easy, Intermediate or Difficult. There are also those plants which are more difficult to bloom in the city than in the country. We list below those we consider Intermediate or Difficult. All the other plants in our blooming plants list are Easy.

	CITY	COUNTRY
Abutilon	Intermediate	Intermediate
Acalypha	Difficult	Intermediate
Achimenes	Difficult	Intermediate
Anthurium	Intermediate	Intermediate
Aphelandra	Difficult	Difficult
Begonia, rhizomatous	Intermediate	Intermediate
Begonia, prismatocapoa	Intermediate	Intermediate
Bougainvillea glabra	Difficult	Intermediate
Browallia	Intermediate	Intermediate

	CITY	COUNTRY
Christmas Cacti	Intermediate	Intermediate
Carissa	Intermediate	Intermediate
Clerodendron	Difficult	Difficult
Crassula schmidtii	Intermediate	Intermediate
Dipladenia	Difficult	Difficult
Fuchsia	Difficult	Intermediate
Gardenia	Intermediate	Intermediate
Geraniums	Difficult	Difficult
Jacobinia	Intermediate	Intermediate
Jasminum Sambac	Intermediate	Intermediate
Jatropha	Intermediate	Intermediate
Lagerstroemia	Intermediate	Intermediate
Malpighia	Intermediate	Intermediate
Nerium	Intermediate	Intermediate
Ochna	Intermediate	Intermediate
Orchids we list	Intermediate	Intermediate
Plumbago	Intermediate	
Primrose	Difficult	Intermediate
Sonerila	Intermediate	Intermediate
Sprekelia	Intermediate	
Stephanotis	Difficult	Intermediate

2. TEMPERATURE REQUIREMENTS FOR BLOOM

Most of the plants we recommend require a minimum of sixty-five degrees F. day or night in order to initiate maximum flowering. They can be maintained in health at five or ten degrees lower, but remember that bloom is our objective.

A few plants which prefer lower temperatures or require higher ones are listed below.

Abutilon megapotamicum (*hybridum*, etc.)	Minimum 60 degrees
Aphelandra squarrosa	Minimum 70 degrees
Fuchsias	Minimum 50 degrees
Geraniums	Minimum 50 degrees
Hibiscus	Minimum 70 degrees
Jasminum sambac	Minimum 70 degrees
Orchids we list	Minimum 55 degrees
Primroses	Minimum 50 degrees
Roses	Minimum 50 degrees

3. Watering for Maintenance and Bloom

The majority of our plants like the soil evenly moist summer and winter. Those having a true rest period go completely waterless during dormancy (see list page 58) while others mostly are watered somewhat less in winter. Listed below are those plants which are exceptional in requiring different treatment summer and winter, or that need wet or dryish conditions at all times.

	SPRING AND SUMMER	WINTER
Abutilon megapotamicum	Freely	Sparingly
Allophyton mexicanum	Wet	Wet
Begonia, rhizomatous	Dryish	Dryish
Christmas Cacti	Dry in the fall	
Clerodendron	Moist	Dry
Clivia	Moist	Dry
Coleus	Sparingly	Sparingly
Crassula schmidtii		
Dipladenia	Moist	Sparingly
Epiphyllum	Moist	Sparingly
Euphorbia bojeri	Wet	Wet
Fuchsia	Moist	Dryish
Geraniums	Dryish	Dryish
Gesneria	Wet	Wet
Haemanthus	Moist	Dry
Haworthia	Moist	Dryish
Jacobinia	Dryish	Dryish
Lantana	Wet	Wet
Manettia	Wet	Moist
Nerine	Dry	Wet
Oxalis	Wet	Wet
Plumbago	Moist	Dryish
Rhoeo	Wet	Wet
Scilla	Moist	Dryish
Sprekelia	Moist	Dry
Stephanotis	Moist	Dryish
Vallota	Dry	Moist

Part 2

Blooming Plants Indoors
Recommended List and
Cultural Directions

In this alphabetical list, Begonias, bromeliads, gesneriads and orchids are grouped together under their respective heads; the rest are arranged alphabetically in individual sequence. Many more plants are discussed under each entry than the one heading it. If you are in any way confused, just consult the index for the page number of the plant you seek.

· *Abutilon megapotamicum. Malvaceae.* South America. Flowering Maple. A summer-flowering plant more suitable for windowsill than light garden. *Can* be everblooming under lights.

Buy in spring for bloom
HEIGHT OR LENGTH: branches 12 to 15
   inches
COLOR: red and yellow
HABIT: hanging
LIGHT: bright indirect
TEMPERATURE: minimum 60 degrees F.
MOISTURE: wet in summer, dryish in
   winter
TRIMMING: in spring, when young,
   and in fall
PROPAGATION: stem cuttings in fall

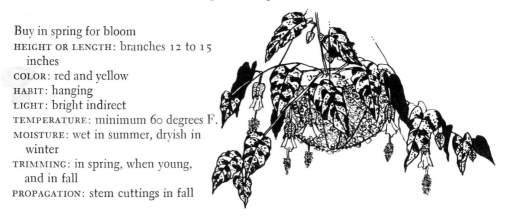

More often cultivated than A. *megapotamicum, Abutilon hybridum* is a plant we have always thought took up much more room than it was worth, unless very carefully trained and cultured. Pale leaves match the pale flowers in various shades of white, yellow and mauve. The flowers are not just pendant; they droop like small, tired mallows. *Hybridum* grows canes up to five feet in height in a single season from a rooted plant and is best in tubs on bright sun porches out of direct sunlight. Definitely not a windowsill plant, and obviously not for the light garden, it must be mentioned because it is certainly quite easy to bloom.

Abutilon megapotamicum is also a fast grower. But at least the canes are weak and it hangs down so that it will not become so large or grow through the top of your light garden. It is also easier to trim and the flowers are much brighter and perkier. The variety 'Aureum' has leaves irregularly spotted with yellow. Numerous three-quarter-inch to

63

one-and-a-half-inch flowers consist of a cupped calyx in bright red with a skirt of yellow petals peeking out, somewhat like a Fuchsia. Because of its hanging habit it must be kept either in a basket, a hanging pot, or, if under the lights, in a pot which is raised to allow the branches to droop somewhat.

A four-inch pot may be sufficient at the start, but later on the heavy roots may take up a ten-inch basket or azalea pot; that depends on how big you want it to grow. Use Light Mix without lime. Keep out of direct sunlight except in the city and six inches from fluorescent tubes. Maintain normal house temperatures of sixty degrees F. or higher with a minimum of forty percent humidity. Soak well in summer but keep just moist in winter. Fertilize with 20–20–20 or other balanced solutions.

Brown leaves result from dry air or excessive sun, while a general loss of leaves is usually due to spider mite. If you suspect these, hang a No-Pest Strip nearby or wash the plant in lukewarm water every three days for two weeks. A single treatment of a soil pesticide will be an added protection (Isotox or VC-13, for instance).

Plants of this type should be ruthlessly trimmed when young, whereupon they produce more shoots, branches, and eventually flowers. By keeping the canes no longer than twelve or fifteen inches, you will have a neat, handsome, colorful plant.

On the windowsill or sun porch A. *megapotamicum* goes into semi-dormancy in the fall and watering must be reduced, otherwise rot will set in. But under lights, as long as the temperature is kept well above the minimum, bloom can continue unabated for much of the winter. In any event, take cuttings of young wood and root them in moist vermiculite so that you have replacement plants ready. Any time of year when the plant is in active growth is all right for propagation, in spite of much advice to the contrary.

A. *striatum* 'Thompsonii' resembles A. *hybridum* with red-veined orange flowers. It starts to bloom when only four or five inches high, but can grow as tall as A. *hybridum*.

• *Acalypha hispida. Euphorbiaceae.* East Indies. Chenille Plant. A largish window plant with showy red cattails.

Buy in spring for bloom
HEIGHT: to 4 or more feet in year
COLOR OF BLOOM: reddish
HABIT: erect
LIGHT: bright sun
TEMPERATURE: minimum 65 degrees F.
MOISTURE: evenly moist
TRIMMING: remove stem tip when
  young to induce branching
PROPAGATION: cuttings in fall

Here is a plant which likes it really warm and humid—not ideal, therefore, for most homes. Cuttings taken in the fall and potted up after rooting in Light Mix will bloom with long red cattails in spring and summer. Discard the old plant the next fall and get going with the cuttings for the following year's bloom. Keep evenly moist. *Acalypha* is very subject to spider mite so keep a No-Pest Strip handy. Best results are achieved on warm sun porches in the country, where it often grows into a very large specimen plant (three to five feet). Given a bright exposure, it can be very showy indeed.

• *Allophyton mexicanum. Scrophulariaceae.* Central America. Mexican Foxglove. Virtually stemless plant for window or light garden or terrarium with good humidity.

Buy for bloom at any time
HEIGHT: maximum 4 inches
COLOR OF BLOOM: purple
HABIT: leafy rosette
LIGHT: partial shade
TEMPERATURE: minimum 60 degrees F.
MOISTURE: always moist
PROPAGATION: seeds or division

Mexican Foxglove displays a complex rosette of four- or five-inch shiny leaves close to the ground and sends up naked stems topped with a cluster of buds which open one by one into small purplish flowers reminiscent of small lobelias.

Culturally it is an easy plant, requiring only warmth and plenty of water. With a little experience you will observe that some plants like it wet and others dryish and that some plants, wet or dry, actually drink more than others. *Allophyton* is always thirsty and consumes water at a rapid rate. We often keep the saucer full of water, and nothing seems to debilitate it as much as any drying out whatsoever.

As the leaves form a pile only an inch or so high and the stem grows only about four inches, it fits well in a terrarium. We find it usually does best when it has plenty of room for roots, so a four-inch pot is called for. Rich Mix, normal balanced fertilizer, and a position within twelve inches of the lights will bring it into bloom. Don't let the temperature fall below sixty degrees F. if you want it to flower. Once started, it blooms pretty freely for a long time.

Hard little erect seed pods are formed and seeds can be collected. But often we simply take a rosette and root it like any other cutting.

In the window, give it partial sunlight in the city in summer. It will bloom only seasonally unless supplementary light is provided in winter. In the light garden it flowers throughout the year.

Anthurium scherzerianum. Araceae. Central America. Flamingo Flower. Windowsill, light garden or terrarium. Everblooming.

Buy for bloom any time
HEIGHT: 6 to 8 inches
COLOR OF BLOOM: red, orange, pink, white or spotted
HABIT: erect
LIGHT: bright indirect
TEMPERATURE: minimum 65 degrees F.
MOISTURE: always moist
PROPAGATION: by division

Around Christmastime you see in the flower shops as cut flowers long-stemmed Anthuriums with enormous red or pink heart-shaped spathes which seem to be lacquered and which last for weeks. A. *scherzerianum* is that plant seen from the wrong end of a telescope—for it has been dwarfed to an eight- to twelve-inch plant with three-inch spathes. The flowers of Anthuriums are minute and cover the spadix, which is the "jack" in the pulpit. The spathe is equivalent to the pulpit—really a big spread-out sheath. But since it is the most colorful part, we think of it as the flower. It doesn't matter. It is to our eyes the flower and is very brilliant and beautiful. A. *scherzerianum*, depending upon variety, can have spathes in red, pink, white, orange or spotted.

As Anthuriums grow under the forest canopy in the tropics, they need very little light. Never set them in sunlight. At the side of a window out of direct rays, at the ends of the tubes in the light garden or in a terrarium planted on the lowest level is the place they require. They must always be kept moist. Even a day of dryness can be lethal. They must have a very porous soil. You can use either osmunda or fern chunks, as for orchids, or pot up in Light Mix without compacting it. They love high humidity but can do without it. If the pot is in an area of low humidity, the soil will dry out very quickly and daily watering will be a must. Use a balanced fertilizer in a very mild dilution once a month and only *after* the medium has been moistened with plain water. The roots are very sensitive and burn easily if subjected to concentrated fertilizer. Maintain sixty-five degrees F. or higher at all times.

The growth of A. *scherzerianum* is from a short stem which is actually the top of the root. The leaves are stemmed and spear-shaped—rather leathery. A plant growing in high humidity will become somewhat larger than one grown in a dryish atmosphere. It appreciates misting.

As the plant develops it forms subsidiary stems with root, which can be pulled off the parent plant. Repot every year and be sure to allow plenty of room as this is one plant which does not like to be cramped.

Given these simple conditions A. *scherzerianum* is reliable and very beautiful. The individual flowers sometimes last for two months.

Aphelandra squarrosa. Acanthaceae. Zebra Plant. Brazil. General-purpose plant but actually requires special handling. Chronic bloomer.

Buy for bloom in spring
HEIGHT: 15 inches
COLOR OF BLOOM: yellow
HABIT: erect
LIGHT: bright sun
TEMPERATURE: over 70 degrees F.
MOISTURE: constantly moist, but not
   wet
TRIMMING: prune top after bloom
PROPAGATION: stem cuttings any time

This fleshy exotic with large leaves striped with white and a short, squarish spike of long yellow flowers is included here only because it is very common in flower shops and because it *is* possible to make it behave after a fashion. Its popularity is due, we believe, more to the rather garish foliage than to the flower. But the latter, though rather short-lived, is cupped in almost equally yellow calyxes which are long-lasting. It is a common gift plant and, when bought in bud, does flourish in the average house for a few weeks. Then leaves begin to contort, dry out and drop off. Given care, it goes through a series of weak attempts to reestablish itself. Hopes are raised that it will bloom again, and sometimes, usually by pure luck, it actually does. But in most instances it is a losing battle and eventually you get tired of trying, and out it goes.

The trouble is that *Aphelandra* is a pure greenhouse plant requiring high humidity, high temperatures and constant moisture. Furthermore, the stem tends to keep growing, branching in a rather ugly way after the flowering stalk has been lopped off. It is pretty hopeless-looking if you allow it to get much taller than 15 inches.

Your plant will be bought at a variety store, florist shop or nursery and be usually ten inches high. The soil is ordinary dirt and the plant is a cutting which has been forced under perfect conditions. The shock of moving to your home is like going from a luxury apartment to a desert tent, unless you can meet its needs.

First of all you must find a spot which is pretty warm, at least during the day—around seventy-five degrees; no problem in summer but difficult the rest of the year. While taking care of temperature you must also provide humidity of sixty percent or better. So the plant must be placed near a humidifier or sit atop a bed of wet pebbles or plastic crate. In addition, you should mist it morning and evening and keep it just moist at all times. It thrives in bright reflected light or full sun part of the day in the city. Fertilize regularly with a balanced solution.

Older plants will branch and cuttings can be taken of three or four nodes. Treat the tip with hormone powder and plant with the lowest leaf node submerged in Rich Mix. If room temperature is below seventy-five degrees F., enclose in a plastic bag for two weeks.

Hopefully your cutting will root and you will have an *Aphelandra* which is better acclimated to your house than the old one. You will even be able to reduce humidity and temperature a bit without harming it. The new plant will be good for six to eight months, and then you can start cuttings again. It makes no difference whether you do your cutting in summer or winter, as long as the environment is warm and humid.

Under lights the situation is the same. It can be placed toward the ends of the tubes, some six inches away. Tubes and ballasts will produce enough heat with the room at normal temperatures to keep it happy. Spraying and misting are even more necessary under lights because of the drying effect of the tubes.

If you think *Aphelandra* is worth the trouble you can always have a pot in bloom on your windowsill or in the light garden. But you must either love the challenge or love the plant to be willing to do that.

The plants on the market bear various varietal labels but all behave in very much the same way.

BEGONIAS

There are over five hundred species of Begonias growing in all parts of the world and an even greater number of hybrids. Of those we can grow in the house, which are the majority, almost all can be bloomed but very few have spectacular flowers. What distinguishes this family is its great variety and beauty of foliage shapes and colors. The flowering is a bonus for which we are grateful, and it is impossible to ignore these plants in any list of those that flower indoors.

Although *Begonia* specialists break down the genus into several categories, the ones that really count are called "rhizomatous," "cane" and "fibrous-rooted." Since it is impossible to go into full detail regarding this remarkable family, we will try to present it by means of a few special examples.

Belva Kusler's hybrids are fine examples of modern *Begonia* breeding. Since even the largest-growing of these are worth recommending to indoor growers as juvenile plants, we have listed some of her productions. From this list, we have chosen one cane type *Begonia* and one rhizomatous type, and describe their habit and culture. Then we discuss two fibrous-rooted plants, one a remarkable novelty and the other a very floriferous and common one—*Begonia prismatocarpa* and *Begonia semperflorens* respectively. The famous Rex Begonias, with their extraordinarily beautiful foliage, have a flower which is so small and hidden that it does not belong properly in the category of a blooming house plant.

Small Cane Types

'Jill Adair'. Smooth narrow leaves. Clusters of white flowers. Bushy.

'Victoria Kartack'. Light pinkish-green leaves. Pink flowers all year. Bushy.

Larger Cane Types (some relatively low and compact, others tall)

'Anna Christine'. Black ruffled leaves, red beneath. Coral-red flowers. Spreading.

'Dorothy Barton'. Bronze leaves and clusters of pink flowers. Arching canes. Compact.

'Frances Lyons'. Light green satin leaves. Floriferous. Pink flowers. Compact.

'Freda Stevens'. Olive-green leaves with silver spots. Deep pink flowers. Compact.

'Gigi Fleetham'. Large copper-green leaves. Pink flowers.

'Grace Lucas'. Serrated leaves dotted silver. Pink flowers, arching canes.

'Jeanne Fleetham'. Large, wavy leaves. White flowers.

'Laura Englebert'. Angel-wing leaves. Red flowers. Tall.

'Margaret Stevens'. Olive-green leaves dusted silver. Red flowers. Large plant.

'Nancy Gail'. Copper leaves. Profusion of pink flowers. Compact.

'Peggy Stevens'. Green leaves dusted pink. Pink flowers. Large.

'Rosalie Wahl'. Broad olive-green leaves with silver spots. Pink flowers continuously.

'Sophie Cecile'. Lobed leaves splashed silver. Large clusters of pink flowers. Huge-growing but beautiful when young.

'Swirly Top'. Ruffled copper-green leaves. Large pink flowers.

Rhizomatous Types

'Jean Herr'. Star-shaped leaves spotted silvery pink. Upright. Pink flowers.

'Raquel Wood'. Green leaves, edged and splashed brown. Pink flowers.

In all the cane types the reverses of the leaves are richly colored either pink or red. Mrs. Kusler was particularly successful in causing the leaves of some of the large types to grow closer together, thus shortening the stems. In others she sacrificed this quality to clear bright leaf markings and large flower clusters.

The following cultural suggestions for rhizomatous and a cane type apply also to the *Begonia* species and other hybrids in the same categories.

***Begonia* 'Jean Herr'.** Belva Kusler hybrid. Rhizomatous *Begonia* for windowsill or light garden. Long blooming period.

Buy for bloom in spring
HEIGHT: 10 to 15 inches
COLOR OF BLOOM: pink
HABIT: spreading
LIGHT: bright reflected
TEMPERATURE: minimum 60 degrees F.
MOISTURE: dry between waterings
TRIMMING: trim back rhizome to
    promote spreading
PROPAGATION: rhizome cuttings

The *Begonia* rhizome is a curious feature. It is thick and fleshy, creeping along the top of the soil or lifting itself up a few inches into the air. The underside grows roots into the soil and the top first develops leaves and flowers which, when they are done for, just leave more rhizome behind. When the rhizome of a creeping type climbs over the side of the pot, you have to cut it, let us say in the middle. The front part you can pot up and the back part you may hope will eventually put up leaves again and start crawling. When the climbing type of rhizome gets out of hand, you have to do the same thing. The forward part, which is above the soil, has no root, but if it is laid on moist soil in a humid atmosphere and provided with warmth, it will root again. Cutting off the extreme tip of a rhizome makes it branch. So, handling the rhizome properly is half the solution to keeping the plants shapely. Believe us, it is no cinch. Young plants are much easier to handle than old ones, so always keep cuttings coming along. Nothing is more unsightly than a straggly old rhizomatous *Begonia* with that rhizome hanging at the bottom of the pot and most of soil at the top of the pot bare of covering.

The flowers of these Begonias are borne on an erect stem well above the leaves. They are usually arranged in a loose raceme, are pink or white in color and rather pale. The effect is pretty, though not very showy. Except with respect to *size* of spike and flower, they all look much alike. The cane types are certainly more colorful. What distinguishes the rhizomatous Begonias are their marvelous leaves in many shapes, textures and colorings. The gorgeous Rex Begonias differ in that they bloom below the leaves, but these are grown entirely for their foliage.

All, or almost all, rhizomatous Begonias are similar in their sensitivity to excess watering. One very experienced grower never waters these plants until they begin to droop. Of course, some species and hybrids tolerate more watering than others, but you can treat them all pretty much the same in this respect without risk. The risk is that if you give them too much water just once the rhizome and the leaves will rot. It took us a long time to overcome our fear that these Begonias would die of thirst. They don't. For one thing, the rhizome is a water-storage vessel, and even if a leaf or two should dry out completely, the rhizome will produce new ones as soon as it is watered.

Most rhizomatous Begonias can be grown in good reflected light, or up to fifteen inches from the tubes. But they will bloom better in partial sun and closer to the tubes. Some of the species and hybrids are long-night plants (see page 193). Temperatures of sixty-five degrees F. or higher are advisable. Lower ones are tolerated but then the plants become even more sensitive to moisture.

The effect of high humidity on these Begonias is remarkable. Just put one in a terrarium and you will see the leaves develop to twice the size they would be on the windowsill, with their growth rate accelerating fantastically. If you do move one to a terrarium, don't take the plants out of it without a hardening-off period. The humid environment should be reduced slowly over a period of two weeks. Do it suddenly and the plant will collapse. This only illustrates that, although humidity of over fifty percent is not necessary for growth and health, it is much to be preferred. Dry air will curl the leaves and cause brown spots and edges.

Pot in Rich Mix with lime. When you fertilize, be careful to moisten the soil first and reduce the dilution to ¼ the manufacturer's recommendation. Once a week with a balanced formula is ample.

Begonia 'Jean Herr' is only one of a very large and interesting group of flowering Begonias of the rhizomatous type. It has large, irregular star-shaped leaves in a deep green with silvery-pink spots and the under-part a dark red. The petioles (leaf stems) are rather long. Flowers are pink and unusually attractive for this category of *Begonia*.

Begonia 'Lenore Olivier'. Belva Kusler Hybrid. Cane-type *Begonia* suitable for windowsill or light garden and with intermittent attractive bloom throughout the year.

Buy for bloom any time
HEIGHT: 12 inches
COLOR OF BLOOM: orange-pink
HABIT: erect, curved
LIGHT: partial sun
TEMPERATURE: minimum 65 degrees F.
MOISTURE: constantly moist
TRIMMING: trim back to produce
    branching
PROPAGATION: stem cuttings with leaf

Cane Begonias have stems which grow straight up or arch. Some types produce many stems, others have a tendency to stay single or double. Clusters of flowers hanging down, sometimes on long stems, are larger than those of the rhizomatous Begonias, and the colors, from white to deep pink and red-orange, are much richer. But just as rhizomes get out of hand, so do canes. They do not branch much, if at all, and just keep elongating, until the time comes when they have either grown beyond all reason or exhaust the largest pot. After a while, you just have to start over again from cuttings, which take easily in moist vermiculite.

It is pleasant to report that cane-type Begonias thrive on plentiful watering though you may want them not to grow so fast. They bloom more easily than the rhizomatous types and more often. With the more floriferous species and cultivars you may have bloom on and off all through the year, and the pendant masses of flower last a long time. Incidentally you should note that there are two kinds of flowers, male and female, in all *Begonia* inflorescences. The female ones have a prominent winged ovary behind the petals.

B. 'Lenore Olivier' is a beauty. The leaves, which are a modified angel wing, are six inches long and very dark green, with silver spots and deep red reverse. The young leaves are a bright reddish color as they unfold. The stem is strong and it arches. The leaves are set close together, overlapping. This is due to relatively slow growth and short internodes which keep the whole plant rather compact and extend its useful life.

When 'Lenore Olivier' has spread out six or eight inches long and is about five inches high, it will bloom, the truss of flowers protruding between the front leaves and spreading out close to the tip of the plant. The effect of the closely packed orange-red brilliance is tremendous. The plant takes about a year to grow fifteen or eighteen inches outward and some nine inches tall. Then you can start over again with cuttings, which root very easily.

Although all the cane types seem to be able to live with relatively little light—at the side of the window or well away from the lights—to achieve bloom they need a good deal of light, and we keep 'Lenore Olivier' tip within four or five inches of the tubes. A sunny window is called for in the city, but bright reflected light from south or west is sufficient in the country. High humidity and frequent mistings also help.

These plants are heavier feeders than some other Begonias and can be fertilized with each watering at one-quarter strength of a balanced solution.

Mrs. Kusler has been particularly successful in hybridizing cane Begonias which are relatively compact. However, one of hers, 'Sophie Cecile', will grow eight feet high and produce enormous masses of bloom. That is not the kind you want for your windowsill. So check with the nursery. Ask for compact-growing types, not over two or three feet.

All these Begonias can be potted in Rich Mix with plenty of lime.

· ***Begonia prismatocarpa. Begoniaceae.*** Fibrous-rooted. Everblooming terrarium plant in window or under lights.

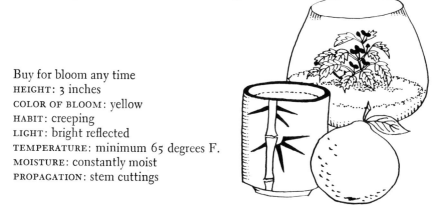

Buy for bloom any time
HEIGHT: 3 inches
COLOR OF BLOOM: yellow
HABIT: creeping
LIGHT: bright reflected
TEMPERATURE: minimum 65 degrees F.
MOISTURE: constantly moist
PROPAGATION: stem cuttings

Most species Begonias bloom only seasonally, and most of them are grown for foliage. But *Begonia prismatocarpa* is a recent introduction which created a sensation for its flowers. Imagine a frilled-leaf angel-wing Begonia, leaf color bright green, creeping only a couple of inches high, and loaded with half-inch two-petaled yellow flowers with red lines radiating from the base. As long as you treat it right, it will never stop blooming. Among the nontuberous Begonias, yellow is a rare color and this one is a good strong chrome shade. For the privilege of buying a little cutting, amateurs have paid the highest prices per square inch of plant that we can remember. Fortunately it is easy to multiply, and there will be plenty of it around shortly.

The requirements are quasi-continuous closure under terrarium conditions. That means that you must use a small fishtank, snifter or other glass container, lay down a base of gravel or lime chips for drainage and fill it part way with Rich Mix very loosely, just moistened but not wet. The plant is set into the soil and the container out of direct sunlight in a bright window, or within five inches of the lights. Fertilize with high phosphate and potash solution every two weeks. The container must have a glass or plastic cover which should be opened only on days when the temperature climbs over eighty degrees F. and the humidity outside is high. Of course, a transparent container should never be placed in full sun or the plants will cook. Water need only be added if the soil inside becomes fairly dry, and then only enough to restore the original moist condition.

In this environment *B. prismatocarpa* grows like mad, blooms so that the flowers almost hide the leaves and spreads by means of nearly aerial roots which come out from every leaf node and bury into the soil. Soon you will have to remove parts of the plant, which are easily broken off, and you can then start new colonies without a regular propagation box—just plant in another snifter or bottle. Long periods of sunless days will, of course, stop blooming and the temperature should never drop below sixty degrees F. If any mildew develops, an annoyance I have not experienced, mist the plants with a solution of Dupont "Benlate."

You will love this small, unique plant.

· **Begonia semperflorens. Begoniaceae.** Wax Begonias. Hybrids. Fibrous-rooted. Floriferous and easy Begonias for window or light garden.

Buy for bloom any time
HEIGHT: 6 to 12 inches
COLOR OF BLOOM: white, pink, red
HABIT: fleshy branching
LIGHT: bright reflected to full sun
TEMPERATURE: minimum 60 degrees F.
MOISTURE: constantly moist
TRIMMING: trim top to promote
    spreading
PROPAGATION: stem cuttings

Those massed plantings you see in public gardens are all one or another variety of Wax Begonia. It is strange that they are not used more often as edging plants in private gardens, for they flower right through the hot, dry spells of an American summer. Indoors they bloom at any time of the year and have only one serious drawback. While they thrive planted in the open in the worst kind of soil and remain dwarfed, in the house, with better treatment, they can get awfully leggy. At least most of them do. If you keep pinching back the new growth to encourage bushiness they can be very satisfactory, and one of the best plants for a beginner.

Seeds should be planted on the surface of the mix as they need light for germination, which takes place in about fifteen days. Six weeks later you should have your first bloom. By that time you will have transplanted it from the propagation box to a small pot whence it can be moved to larger ones as it grows.

Use Rich Mix with lime and try to keep the plant potbound. Vegetative growth is what you do not want. By giving *semperflorens* high phosphate-potash fertilizer once a week you will have sufficient bloom. It likes water but drying out between will maintain its bushiness. The more light you give it the more compact it will remain, but it will tolerate reflected sunlight and a position on the side of your light garden within about 6 inches of the tubes.

After six months of bloom the fleshy stems begin to sag even if you have pruned it well. So, if you like the particular plant, start new ones with cuttings. Otherwise plant new seed.

The flowers themselves hardly need description. They are two-petaled and the colors are usually rather watery. Double varieties, with flowers like untidy rosebuds, are preferred by some. Since there are so many hybrids on the market, one occasionally runs across very pure whites or strong apricot shades which are more attractive than the run-of-the-mill plants. And, occasionally, one of your plants will be more consistently dwarfed. Propagate such plants, as they are not plentiful and are of a somewhat different type than the preferred outdoor plant.

In the seed catalogues you will see listings of numerous varieties. we like 'Linda,' a heavily flowering pink dwarf, and the larger Organdy strain in several colors. Paris Market, Butterfly and the rosebud doubles are twelve-inch plants. You will have to experiment a bit until you find those which suit your conditions. Calla Lily Begonias are *semperflorens*

Begonias with variegated white-and-green leaves. They are subject to fungal diseases and are more sensitive to heavy watering. Grow them rather dry.

Since Wax Begonias attract all the standard insects, a No-Pest Strip hung in the neighborhood is a sensible preventive.

Bougainvillea glabra. Nyctaginaceae. Brazil. Bougainvillea. Shrubby or vining plant for sun porch or windowsill. Spring bloomer.

Buy plants for bloom in spring
HEIGHT: 2 to 3 feet in the house
COLOR OF BLOOM: purple, red, pink
HABIT: bushy, trailing
LIGHT: full sun
TEMPERATURE: minimum 65 degrees F.
MOISTURE: moist spring and summer; dryish in winter
TRIMMING: trim in spring for bushiness, and drastically in September
PROPAGATION: stem cuttings in early spring

Bougainvillea is one of the glories of the tropics. They are big vines which, like Clematis in the North, attach themselves to and cover the sides of buildings with flaming masses of flower. Because of their beauty there has always been, despite their size, a great temptation to grow them indoors, especially on sun porches. This is not easy because of their need for bright sunlight and the rapidity of growth.

There has been a considerable amount of hybridization with the object of making *Bougainvillea* shrubby, but it still remains a pretty big plant. B. 'Barbara Karst' with red bracts (the flowers are tiny; it is the bracts that supply the color) is relatively tamable and the oldest of these crosses. The more recent 'Texas Dawn' is a beautiful pink, and 'Spectabilis', probably the best for our purposes, is purple and the longest-blooming. The plants are offered at spring flower shows and in garden centers as two-foot-high plants in six-inch pots—which is already rather large. Unlabeled varieties are a distinct gamble. All the newer strains are less thorny than their predecessors.

The plants are shipped from Southern nurseries in ordinary soil, which, after the plant has a rest, should be washed off and replaced with Rich Mix without lime. Choose a pot allowing ample room for roots, and if there arc long canes, even in bloom, cut them back to half their length to strengthen the plant and make it branch. Then put it in the sunniest spot of your sunniest window and feed it with a high-nitrate fertilizer at every watering, using thc full strength recommended by the manufacturer. Keep it above sixty-five degrees F. during its spring-to-summer flowering period.

In a warm plant room we have grown cuttings to bloom in winter directly under the lights. The very attractive and long-lasting bloom is worth the effort. But growth is difficult to control, and the vines get in the way of everything else. Further experimentation may show that we can bush the plant under lights. Otherwise you must think of it as a big plant for a sunny location, preferably with supplementary artificial light.

Since it is such a rapid grower you may have to trellis it after a couple of months. When its dormant period starts in September, prune it back severely, almost like a rosebush. At the same time, reduce watering so that the plant dries out well in between and eliminate fertilizing entirely. In January you can start the spring regimen again. Mealybugs and scale can be prevented by hanging a No-Pest Strip nearby.

BROMELIADS. *Bromeliaceae.* Tropical America. Air Plants.

The family *Bromeliaceae* is found only in the American tropics where it grows in immense numbers on tree limbs and occasionally on rocks. The roots of these plants are used mainly for attachment, and feeding is principally through their leaves. Hence their common name of "air plants." Both Spanish Moss and the Pineapple plant belong to this unusual family.

Many of the plants are urn-shaped, their centers adapted to hold water. The flowers of most species are rather small and of short duration, while the bright coloration of the leafy bracts which surround them may last for months. Foliage is often striped or zoned attractively and the lower parts of leaves turn flaming red at bloom time. Finally, some plants have berries following their flowering which may also persist for months. Bromeliads are among the easiest plants to grow and bloom. So, all in all, though flowering in most species occurs only once a year, they deserve their popularity. In fact, the supply of good plants is less than the demand. The culture of bromeliads is pretty much the same for the different species and cultivars.

Like orchids, bromeliads only bloom from new growths, which appear either from the side or the center of the old plant. The parent dies off eventually and the new ones take over. Where growth is from the center you may remove the old leaves as they brown off. Cut off half-grown side growths at the basal joint along with root and pot them up separately.

The best media are those usually prescribed for orchids: osmunda, tree fern or fir bark mixtures—all available from orchid nurseries. They will also do all right in Rich Mix without lime. Some of the smaller plants will do best if attached by means of wire to a slab of tree fern. Pots can be smaller than for most other plants since bromeliad rooting is well below the average. A four- or five-inch pot will hold the biggest of the usual ones in cultivation.

When you have bought a young plant or separated a sucker, grow it in moderate light, on the side of a windowsill—east, west or south—or five to eight inches from the light. The main thing from there on is to keep the urn-shaped foliage full of water and, if there is no urn, to spray the leaves once or twice daily. Water will trickle down to the roots. Do not soak the potting medium, as the base of the plant is liable to rot. Once a month, treat the plants to a very mild solution of a high-nitrate fertilizer or fish emulsion. Temperature should be 65 degrees F. or better at all times. High humidity (over 50 percent) is very beneficial.

The main challenge is getting them to flower. A few will perform without any special treatment—Queen's Tears (*Billbergia nutans*) or *Cryptanthus*, for instance—but most of them need something to trigger the growth of a blooming stem. The time to do this is when the new plant is mature—in other words, as big as your older plant, or like other blooming plants you have seen at nurseries or florist shops. Bromeliad books with illustrations show how a mature plant should look. Having satisfied yourself on this point, encase your plant in a plastic bag along with half an apple for four days. Make sure that the bag is airtight. Six weeks or less after this treatment the flowering shoot will appear. A chemical is on the market which will accomplish the same thing, but apples are available everywhere and, unless you have a large collection of bromeliads, using these is the easier way. Moving your plant to your brightest lighted position when the stalk appears will contribute to the intensity of bract coloring. For those bromeliads whose flowering takes place in the urn itself, the beginning of coloration in the surrounding leaves is your best sign of oncoming bloom.

Bromeliads occasionally attract scale. On flat-leaved plants, you can remove them with a brush dipped in alcohol. With the more contorted types, dipping in malathion may be necessary. The plant should be well washed off a day after the dip. But a No-Pest Strip nearby will prevent the scale in the first place.

Cool temperatures cause bromeliads to rot. Enclose small species in a terrarium where they will benefit from the high humidity and grow extremely well.

· *Aechmea fasciata. Bromeliaceae.*　　Urn Plant. Window and light garden (if you have the space).

Buy for bloom in bud
HEIGHT: 2 feet
COLOR OF BLOOM: pink and blue
HABIT: erect
LIGHT: partial sun
TEMPERATURE: minimum 65 degrees F.
MOISTURE: fill cup at all times; spray
　often
PROPAGATION: by division

You have probably seen this startling plant bloom in florist shops, usually in February and March. The gray-green-and-white striped leaves form a magnificent whorl from which the thick stem rises straight up, topped by something like a decorative sundae of blue flowers surrounded by pink spiky bracts. The bracts retain their color up to five months long. It is a big plant, some eighteen to twenty-four inches across and about fifteen inches high. It needs all the room it can get because its leaves are stiff and can't be crowded. This is not the easiest of the bromeliads and we recommend the best light you can give it unless the leaves show the effect of burn. The leaf color is more brilliant in good light.

Another *Aechmea*, 'Foster's Favorite', has burgundy-red leaves and blue flowers. Its habit is more erect than *fasciata's*. Blue berries last for several months. It is also easier than *fasciata*, but not so gorgeous.

• *Tillandsias. Bromeliaceae.*   Tropical America. Window or light garden. Seasonal bloomers.

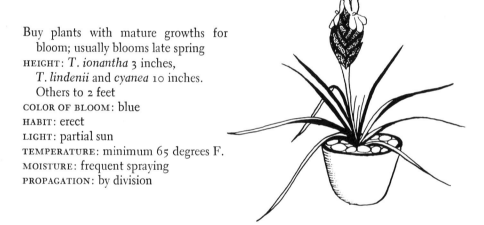

Buy plants with mature growths for
    bloom; usually blooms late spring
HEIGHT: *T. ionantha* 3 inches,
    T. lindenii and *cyanea* 10 inches.
    Others to 2 feet
COLOR OF BLOOM: blue
HABIT: erect
LIGHT: partial sun
TEMPERATURE: minimum 65 degrees F.
MOISTURE: frequent spraying
PROPAGATION: by division

There are many possibilities for house culture in this largest of bromeliad genera. Many of them are quite small plants and are more common than and not as expensive as the big fellows, which are getting somewhat prohibitive in price, since they take a long time to grow to market. Some Tillandsias have papery leaves, others fleshy ones with roundish cross section. The latter make wonderful subjects for a dome terrarium. The flowers are mostly small; some are exquisitely perfumed and all have pretty long-lasting bracts; the plants don't need a great deal of light and culture is easy. The main thing is to spray them early and often.

Tillandsia ionantha is a great favorite which has a thick tuft of hard, dry foliage; it is only three inches high, and really blushes when ready to bloom in the spring. The flowering stalk bears small blue flowers. If you spray it daily it can be grown attached with wire to a little tree-fern raft (see page 80).

Tillandsia lindenii is a bigger plant with thin quill-like leaves, making a spread which may be as much as fifteen inches. In early spring the spike produces a flat inflorescence whose bracts are a vivid pink and the flowers, exceptionally large, are blue. *Tillandsia cyanea* is similar.

Vriesia. Bromeliaceae. Tropical America. Window and light garden. Seasonal bloomer.

Buy in bud for bloom
HEIGHT: 18 inches
COLOR OF BLOOM: red bracts
HABIT: erect
LIGHT: partial sun
TEMPERATURE: minimum 65 degrees F.
MOISTURE: fill cups and spray regularly
PROPAGATION: by division

The Vriesias are admired for their richly colored or zoned leaves and their floral spikes whose chief beauty is the brilliance of their overlapping bracts.

Vriesia splendens. Flaming Sword. These plants are about twenty inches in diameter with dark-green and light-green striped leaves. The inflorescences are tall spears colored in brilliant red or orange. Flowers are inconspicuous. A long-lasting show.

· **Browallia. Solanaceae.** Tropical America. Annual plant, better in the light garden than in the window. For baskets on the sun porch.

Buy for bloom in spring
HEIGHT: 10 inches
COLOR OF BLOOM: blue or white
HABIT: erect to spreading
LIGHT: partial sun
TEMPERATURE: minimum 60 degrees F.
MOISTURE: constantly moist
TRIMMING: trim for bushy growth
PROPAGATION: seed or stem cuttings in
   the fall

Blue is as scarce and welcome indoors as out. There seem to be innumerable red, yellow and white flowers, but the blues are always in the minority. All the better that we can borrow a few from the annuals, which we are at last able to raise indoors because of fluorescent light. True, Browallia and similar plants do all right in a sunny window, but stretches of cloudy days will set them back and they will bloom again only if there is a long period of bright light. That is why supplementary artificial light makes such a difference.

Seeds are offered by all the major seed companies in variously labeled shades of blue and white. The object has been to produce more compact plants, less tending to straggle in garden borders or in pots. Some progress has been made in this respect, although stems still are rather lax. Accordingly they must be grown in a basket, set on an inverted pot or kept drastically trimmed.

Seed in September for winter bloom. Fifteen days are required for germination. Always plant on top of the soil where the seed receives bright light. A couple of half-grown seedlings can be potted in a four-inch pot in Light Mix and placed in a bright window or under the lights. Nip them as soon as they have several leaves and continue to do so as they mature to encourage a lot of branching. The height of the plants should not be over eight inches.

Soon large, five-lobed chalice flowers will appear in great numbers in the axils and make a brave show. The plants are indifferent to house temperatures and need only regular watering and fertilizer. Just don't soak them excessively. Bloom should last all winter. *Browallia* stays about ten to twelve inches high but spreads. Cut back excess branching.

Plants grown in the garden can be brought indoors in the fall, pruned, potted up leaving room for new roots, and treated like the fall seed-grown plants. You can take some cuttings at the same time, root them and discard the old plants (which may be a little tired) when the new ones start to bloom.

Carissa grandiflora nana compacta. Apocynaceae. South Africa. Natal Plum. Slow-growing plant for window or light garden. Off-and-on bloomer.

Buy for bloom in spring
HEIGHT: keep to 6 inches
COLOR OF BLOOM: white
HABIT: bushy
LIGHT: full sun
TEMPERATURE: minimum 65 degrees F.
MOISTURE: constantly moist
TRIMMING: prune to encourage
  branching
PROPAGATION: stem cuttings in fall

In Florida, *Carissa* is widely used as a hedge. With its very branching habit and closely packed fleshy, dark-green, nearly round leaves, it forms a solid mass. Invisible from a distance are the long spines, which make it even more effective than barberry as a barrier. But then it flowers too, with lovely fragrant two-inch white blooms followed by a one-inch brilliant red fruit from which the locals make a jelly. In the house the outdoor *Carissa* will grow much too big, and bloom is unlikely.

Instead, you should get the form *nana compacta*, sometimes called Bonsai Carissa, which has a nearly horizontal growth, the leaves opposite on fairly heavy branches. Because of its slow growth and tolerance of continuous pruning it makes a most attractive bonsai plant, which, with some care, will even bloom and fruit. As a foliage plant it requires only moderate light—well at the side of the window or the light garden. But if you want bloom you must set it in full sun or at the center of the lights. In fact, in the window it should have supplemental illumination.

In regard to soil it is rather indifferent. We have potted it in Cactus and Succulent or Light Mix, both with lime, achieving about equally good results. And we keep it potbound to reduce the rate of growth. Probably we would be better off to grow it with more room and ultimately have a good-sized leafy plant. But we like it small. So few of the plants in our repertory have this talent for woody compactness that *Carissa* is something to cherish. It is enormously decorative in a Japanese pot.

Humidity is not important but, though *Carissa* can stand temperatures down to freezing, it will not bloom in the house at less than sixty-five degrees F. It needs very little balanced fertilizer—once a month at most. As for producing fruit, you need either bees or to do your own pollination, as it will not do the job by itself. Keep moist, but not wet, at all times.

Propagate in moist vermiculite by means of stem cutttings of the light-green new growth.

• **Citrus Plants. Rutaceae.**   China. Ideal house plants for window or light garden. Flowers and fruit all year round.

Buy for bloom any time
HEIGHT: 2 to 3 feet
COLOR OF BLOOM: white
HABIT: shrubby
LIGHT: bright reflected
TEMPERATURE: minimum 65 degrees F.
MOISTURE: constantly moist
TRIMMING: after bloom to maintain compact shape
PROPAGATION: stem cuttings in the fall

Citrus trees are deservedly popular house plants as they bloom fragrantly on and off throughout the year and produce fruits which, if not particularly edible when home-grown, are very ornamental. The question is which of the available plants is best and easiest. The horticultural varieties are all dwarf and the culture is the same for all. *Citrus auranti-*

folia (the Key Lime), *Citrus* 'Meyeri' and *Citrus taitensis* (Otaheite Orange), are all good plants. Personally we opt for the Nagami Kumquat, which is a very manageable shrub, much branched, with fragrant white flowers and oval, orange-colored edible fruits. In the city it requires the brightest sunlight to flower and fruit but in the country can be placed in reflected or partial sunlight. It should be regularly pruned and trained for best appearance in the house and for convenience in the light garden.

As these are long-lived plants, it is advisable to buy them as juveniles. Those bought from Florida nurseries or shipped from there should be quarantined from your other plants because they often carry scale and other insects. Examine the leaves closely for pests, especially along the veins. Also, the soil used is often of poorest quality and not suitable for house-plant culture. After your plant has become acclimated and is judged free of insects, it should be knocked out of its pot and the soil washed off completely in lukewarm water.

Repot carefully in a larger container, spreading the roots and making sure that the soil is solidly packed. Use Light Soil Mix *without lime*. After repotting, trim the plant back somewhat and set in low light for a few weeks. Then it can be placed in its permanent location and, after a month, fertilized with high-nitrogen solution (30–10–10) and given a dose of chelated iron (Sequestrene). Allow to dry out between waterings. From there on your shrub will do well. House temperature and humidity variations are of no consequence.

As the Kumquat shrub grows older it may need bonsai treatment. In order to keep it in check (one to two feet) and well shaped, it is necessary to cut off excess root and trim back the top growth at the same time before replanting. Treated in this way once every couple of years, it can last for a very long time and provide continuous pleasure.

Clerodendron thomsoniae. Verbenaceae. West Africa. Glory Bower. A Blooming vine for country window or light garden. Bloom from spring to fall.

Buy for bloom in March
HEIGHT: length of stems is interminable; maintain at 12 to 15 inches by pruning
COLOR OF BLOOM: white and red
HABIT: vine
LIGHT: full sun
TEMPERATURE: minimum 65 degrees F.
MOISTURE: moist February–November; dry November–February
TRIMMING: prune drastically to keep short and bushy
PROPAGATION: young stem cuttings, June to September

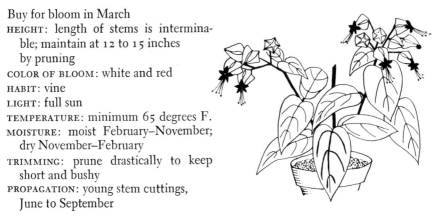

The flowering of *Clerodendron* consists of big trusses of snow-white calyces which are fluted and cupped and from which the blood-red five-petaled corolla seems to extrude and spread over the surface. There is certainly no more beautiful vine for the house. Given a big tub in a greenhouse it will grow to enormous size, but it can be kept quite small by seasonal pruning, becoming more shrublike in growth. It is not ever-blooming because it needs a controlled rest in winter, even under artificial light. We have not seen it bloom in a city window. However, in the country and the light garden it flowers from March to November, which is certainly sufficient.

Blooming a *Clerodendron* indoors involves selecting the right plant. Unfortunately there is no guaranteed-to-bloom strain available at nurseries. We had to try out quite a number before we hit on one which performed as it should. In our window one of the plants that failed to bloom still grows vigorously. But the plant which finally bloomed now lives in our light garden and we propagate it for friends. The only visible difference we can note in this plant is that the leaves are somewhat more quilted and of heavier texture. In the case of *Clerodendron*, experimenting is well worthwhile, for once you have hit upon the right one you will be rewarded with years of magnificent bloom.

Usually it is bought as a single-stemmed or two-branched juvenile eight or ten inches high. Acquire it in the spring in bud or flower so that you can enjoy it through a season.

If potted in ordinary soil, wash this off and transplant into Rich Soil Mix with lime. Set it in your sunniest window in the city and you may have luck. In the country it should be out of prolonged direct sunlight. Under the lights it must be within ten inches of the tubes. Keep it just moist and never let it dry out completely. During the blooming season give it high phosphate and potash fertilizer solution. Humidity of fifty percent or over encourages bloom. It does well at ordinary room temperature.

Let blooming branches grow but cut off any light-green suckerish growth. These you can root in moist vermiculite to start new plants.

In November reduce watering gradually until the pot finally dries out. Place it in a shaded, preferably cool, place. All the leaves will die off but the stems will remain green. Because home conditions are drier than a greenhouse it is advisable to spray the branches once a week, but do not water.

About the end of February repot the plant in fresh, dry mix and prune it back severely leaving just one stem and a few short branches. It should be no more than eight or ten inches high after the first year. Place it in the light and just moisten the mix, at the same time packing it down firmly and adding more if necessary. After a few days, increase watering. As soon as green growth appears you can start fertilizing. Almost before the leaves are fully out the flowering peduncles will appear.

Unless you want a large shrub, keep *Clerodendron* potbound. Our largest pot is usually a deep five-incher. In time you can train this plant to be a little tree, with a thick stem and a mass of branches each of which will produce flower clusters.

Clerodendron is sometimes spelled *Clerodendrum* Having found it both ways on various authoritative lists we tossed a coin. *Dendron* means treelike in Greek (according to *Botanical Latin* by Stearn).

Clerodendron fragrans is another fine plant which is more shrubby and carries pink clusters. The color is not that showy but it is a neat plant and does not require the dry rest period. Otherwise treat it like *C. thomsoniae*.

Clivia miniata. Amaryllidaceae. South Africa. Kaffir Lily. Plant with magnificent flowers but short blooming season in spring. A window plant.

Buy for bloom in February
HEIGHT: 2 feet
COLOR OF BLOOM: orange
HABIT: leaves spreading, flower stalk
   erect
LIGHT: bright shade or 2 to 3 hours of
   sun
TEMPERATURE: minimum 50 degrees F.
MOISTURE: dry September–January,
   moist January–August
PROPAGATION: division

The trouble with all those wonderful plants of the Lily and Amaryllis families is their short period of bloom. Many of these have been the best flowering plants of the previous epoch of indoor growing. But what a joy it is to have plants now which bloom continuously or for very long periods. You must be really infatuated with these bulb plants to care for them a whole year in the house for so short a pleasure. If we grant all this, however, we must admit that *Clivia* has a special magnificence.

It is also exceptional in having fleshy roots instead of a true bulb. At most, the bases of the leaves thicken into a rudimentary bulb. The plant is evergreen, and has broad and strap-shaped leaves forming overlapping series on opposite sides of the plant. From the center rises the thick green stem topped by an umbel of ten to twenty orange flowers in the spring. Occasionally it blooms in the fall, but don't count on it.

Culture is very simple indeed. A single spread of leaves should go into a six-inch pot. Use Rich Mix without lime and pack it very solidly around the plant, being careful not to break the brittle roots. It does not like loose soil, though excellent drainage is essential. Set it a few feet back from any window where it will get a certain amount of direct sunlight—two or three hours will suffice. And wherever it is happy, leave it. Never move it or even turn it. Total immobility is what it needs.

After blooming cut off the stem and water only after the pot has dried out—about once a week. This is the growth period and new leaves will develop. Mist frequently to keep leaves fresh but do not be concerned about aerial humidity. In September stop watering entirely and allow the pot to stay dry until January. Then start slowly watering again. Bloom will appear in February–April.

Clivia likes a temperature over fifty-five degrees F. and requires a minimum of sixty degrees F. to bloom. Follow the seasonal procedure exactly.

In the course of time offsets develop and you may eventually end up with a huge tub with a dozen stems blooming away at one time. But if you choose, you can break the clusters apart and pot them up separately.

Occasional attacks of mite or scale are easily removed by swabbing the leaves, top and bottom, with alcohol or chlorinated water.

Coleus. Labiatae. Africa and Asia. Easy in all situations.

Buy for bloom any time
HEIGHT: 1 foot in the house
COLOR OF BLOOM: lavender, whitish
HABIT: erect
LIGHT: partial sun—better color with
  brighter light
TEMPERATURE: minimum 50 degrees F.
MOISTURE: evenly moist
TRIMMING: pinch back for compactness
PROPAGATION: stem cuttings any time,
  or seed

Here we are cheating a bit in order to include a genus which occasionally has truly gorgeous foliage. The flowers are hardly sensational but they are certainly easy to come by. Actually the flower spike is much like that of the mints, consisting of numerous small flowers either blue or lilac in a spike. On compact plants they do make a cheerful show.

If there is any one species to recommend for bloom it is *C. thyrsoideus*, the Bush Coleus, whose spikes are a nice bright blue. As for the rest, it is pointless to name a variety. There has been so much hybridizing and crossing that different strains are turning up all the time. One picks out the leaf shapes and colors he likes. Some are fringed, others scallop-edged, and the colors and markings are in all shades and designs. The behavior of the plants is fairly uniform and both light garden and windowsill culture are much alike. For the terrarium it is better to watch for single-stemmed, compact shapes as some plants are quite branching.

Coleus has all the easy-growing characteristics of a weed, requiring our Light Mix, moderate watering, temperatures above fifty degrees and medium light conditions. In strong light the colors are often more brilliant, but the plant can tolerate almost anything. Kept a bit pot-bound and pinched back, it won't get out of hand. We starve them so that they last longer and don't grow too big. The flowers appear even with partial sunlight or when the plant is 18 inches under lights.

When you have a plant with the leaf colors you like, propagate it by means of cuttings. The fleshy stems root quickly in moist vermiculite.

Coleus seed must be sown on top of the medium, needing light to germinate. It comes up in about ten days. There are many strains of mixed seed available and you can get some idea of the pattern from the color illustrations in the seed catalogues.

Crassula schmidtii. Crassulaceae. South Africa. Window or light garden. Summer–fall bloomer.

Buy for bloom in May
HEIGHT: rosette 3 inches maximum;
   flowering stalk 12 inches maximum
COLOR OF BLOOM: red
HABIT: fleshy rosette
LIGHT: partial sun
MOISTURE: moist spring to fall; dryish
   in winter
PROPAGATION: by leaves and division

Growing succulents indoors is not difficult, but only a selected few are reliable bloomers and of these a handful have showy flowers. *C. schmidtii* is an exceptionally pretty plant. The leaves are long (one and a half to two inches) ruled triangles packed into thick overlapping rosettes forming mounds an inch or two high. In summer it sends up thick branched stalks and each branch supports a cluster of small, shapely, deep-red flowers. The ten-inch height of the branches with their very numerous flowers is imposing. The flowers are long-lasting and remain colorful after the petals dry out. For such a small plant—a four-inch pot holds a large mature plant—it provides a great show.

Pot it in Light Mix with plenty of lime and give it good sunlight or artificial light. During spring and summer you can keep it quite moist, thus encouraging growth and flowering. Fertilize it with a balanced solution. For flowering, a temperature of sixty-five degrees F. or better is advisable. After the flowers are gone and the stalks die down *C. schmidtii* takes a rest through the winter and should be allowed to dry out well between light waterings. In the house, we have found it is not advisable to leave it without water for more than a few days at a time. But over-watering can cause rapid rot. So be very sparing and watch your plant carefully. Rather let its leaves shrink a bit before giving it moisture than run the risk of ruining the whole plant.

Once mealybug gets a hold on *C. schmidtii* you are really in trouble. Malathion kills the plant overnight. Removing these pests with alcohol and a brush never works. Luckily we have the No-Pest Strip. When you grow this plant hang it nearby, and you won't get mealybugs.

To propagate, peel off outside leaves and stand upright in moist vermiculite under good light. Do this only during the spring or summer when the plant is in active growth. Rooting is rapid.

Crossandra infundibuliformis (also called *undulaefolia*). *Acanthaceae.* India. Perennial for window or under artificial light.

Buy for bloom any time
HEIGHT: to 18 inches
COLOR OF BLOOM: orange
HABIT: erect
LIGHT: partial sun
TEMPERATURE: minimum 65 degrees F.
MOISTURE: constantly moist
TRIMMING: after bloom, to cause
    branching
PROPAGATION: stem cuttings; seeds are
    slow

Few house plants make a finer display than Crossandras, but it was not until we learned how to propagate them ourselves by means of stem cuttings and bring them quickly into bloom that we realized their full potentiality as year-round flowers. Fortunately they are carried by most up-to-date house plant nurseries, usually as rooted plants, and can occasionally be purchased in variety stores. If they have been planted in dirt it is advisable to wash them off and replant them in Rich Mix. Almost invariably ordinary soil will dry out too quickly in the house or be too heavy for the delicate spreading roots.

The unusual flowers of *Crossandra* lack the long tube and over-hanging upper lobe of most *Acanthaceae—Jacobinia*, for instance. Instead, the lobes are splayed on one horizontal plane with three larger ones bracketed by two smaller ones. This gives them a spread of over an inch and, since two or more flowers bloom in a whorl at the same time, the effect is of a circle of soft, pure orange some three inches across.

The closely packed bud spike seems to start blooming at the top but elongates and produces flowers symmetrically upward. A healthy plant may bear a spike three to four inches long with twenty to thirty blooms providing color for three to four weeks. Meanwhile branches will start flowering, and the display continues for months on end, only finishing due to excessive woodinesss or exhaustion of the root system after about a year in the pot.

Growth starts with a basal stem provided with three- to four-inch wavy-edged leaves, apparently hairless, dark green and very oily-shiny. Once the first flower spike starts to bloom, branches appear and increase in number as the plant is trimmed back. *Crossandra* should not be allowed to grow more than fifteen inches high in the house unless you are preparing it for a show. In the tropics it's a three-foot shrubby plant.

A four-and-a-half-inch shallow plastic pot gives it ample room. A 1–1–1 mix with a liberal addition of lime suits it and you should give it regular feeding with a balanced fertilizer (20–20–20). Keep it constantly moist but not waterlogged.

Under artificial light it is satisfied with two twenty-four-inch tubes at a distance of five inches on a sixteen-hour-light day. It then becomes an everblooming plant—one of our best. It will also thrive in a west or south window, but long periods of dark days will inhibit blooming and cause the plant to become straggly.

Try to maintain humidity at forty percent or better as, otherwise, leaves will tend to curl and brown. Sixty-five degrees F. is about the minimum day temperature for bloom.

If you do not remove the spike after flowering, the plant will produce seeds spontaneously. When the spike turns tan-colored, cut it off at the base and dry it out thoroughly. The seeds, one to a flower, which are easily removed from the husks, germinate in ten days in moist vermiculite or sphagnum moss at seventy degrees F.

However, you can have a quicker successsion of sturdier plants by taking cuttings before the branches develop budding spikes. Cut off the new branch at its base, where it joins the stem, and plant it in vermiculite in a propagating box. Rooting will take place in two or three weeks. Pot directly into a four-incher and, within some four weeks, a flowering spike should appear. Thus a succession can be maintained with enough excess to make gifts of these magnificent plants to your friends.

Crossandras are relatively trouble free, not being subject to fungal infections and not appealing as a host to most pests. White fly will occasionally go for them and can be eliminated by a two-day cycle of thorough spraying with lukewarm water, or by dipping. Excessive watering causes the lower leaves to yellow and drop off.

The plants can be put out in a little shade in the garden in summer. They do not seem to thrive in continuous, very strong sunlight and they become unsightly when beaten by rain and wind, as the flowers are quite fragile. All in all, they are better off in the house.

·*Cuphea hyssopifolia. Lythraceae.*   Central America. Elfin Herb. Perennial for window or light garden. Everblooming.

Buy for bloom any time
HEIGHT: 10 inches
COLOR OF BLOOM: purplish pink
HABIT: shrubby
LIGHT: partial shade
TEMPERATURE: minimum 65 degrees F.
MOISTURE: always moist
TRIMMING: clip tips of branches
PROPAGATION: stem cuttings from
    branches any time; self-seeding

We have seen numbers of these plants in nurseries and not once come across it in a home or amateur greenhouse. Obviously the nurseries would not carry it if they did not sell it, so we must assume that we were never in the right place at the right time. It certainly should be popular with the indoor gardener for, though anything but striking, it is a comfortable plant, pretty, always in bloom and terribly easy to grow.

You have probably seen the long spikes of that naturalized plant from Europe, *Lythrum salicaria,* turning our marshy areas purple in August. And you may have grown other Lythrums in the garden (for instance 'Morden's Pink'). Well, *Cuphea hyssopifolia* belongs to the same family, and the individual flowers, with their unequal purple petals, are almost exactly the same as the wild and garden Lythrums. This is a little bush, with innumerable narrow oval opposite leaves and the small flowers growing in the axils (joints). In a big pot (ten inches) it can grow well over a foot high and more across. But in the house we generally keep it in check or even bonsai it so that it is usually not more than eight or ten inches in height or spread.

We pot it in Light Mix with a little lime, in a 4-inch pot, after it has started to bloom in a two-incher. It must be kept constantly moist. It will grow nicely in any exposure except north and can stand direct or partial sun. Under lights it blooms at a distance of fifteen inches. Normal house temperatures agree with it summer and winter. Fertilize with a balanced solution, and your only chore is keeping it neat by trimming and shaking the branches to get rid of the small dead flowers.

Cuphea puts out rather long thin branches on new growth and these, when cut off, should be propagated in moist vermiculite. A couple of weeks is usually sufficient for rooting. I have never grown it from seed but it does produce them spontaneously in great quantities. After the plant has been in bloom for a while, just shake it well over a sheet of white paper and you will find plenty of the little black seeds, which germinate rapidly. Since growth is fairly slow at first, cuttings are preferable.

We have had mites on *Cuphea* but this is a sturdy little plant and you can swish it in a bucket of lukewarm water with or without Kelthane to get rid of these pests.

Selection of indoor growing and blooming plants. (PHOTO BY JEAN MERKEL,
ALBERTS & MERKEL, INC., BOYNTON BEACH, FLA.)

Seemannia latifolia

Paphiopedilum 'Maudiae'

Paphiopedilum concolor

Begonia 'Lenore Olivier'

Begonia, Nematanthus, Streptocarpus, Episcia and *Oxalis*. (PHOTO BY LAURAY OF SALISBURY, SALISBURY, CONN.)

Orchids, bromeliads and other showy house plants. (PHOTO BY JEAN MERKEL, ALBERTS & MERKEL, INC., BOYNTON BEACH, FLA.)

Streptocarpus 'Cobalt Nymph'

Oxalis martiana aureo-reticulata

Sinningia 'Cindy'

Sinningia hybrid by Ted Bona

Episcia 'Acajou'

Miniature *Episcia* 'Jinny Elbert'

Columnea erythrophaea

Clerodendron thomsoniae

Gesneria cuneifolia var. El Yunque

Cuphea platycentra. Lythraceae. Mexico. Cigar Flower. Annual plant for the window or light garden.

Buy for bloom in spring
HEIGHT: 10 inches
COLOR OF BLOOM: red with black tip
HABIT: fleshy, branched
LIGHT: partial sun
TEMPERATURE: minimum 60 degrees F.
MOISTURE: keep wet
TRIMMING: trim when young for
   branching
PROPAGATION: seeds and stem cuttings

The Cigar Flower is a very different plant from its close relative *Cuphea hyssopifolia*. It is a fleshy, branched plant with one- to two-inch leaves pointed at both ends. The flowers are three-quarters-inch-long narrow tubes, flaming red with a black ring on the tip backed up by a white ring. Each flower is held from below by a threadlike springy pedicel. The growth is rather diffuse and the flowers are distributed on all the branches. In the house the plant tends to be rather ungainly, due to an uneven arrangement of just about everything, but the flowers are unusual and pretty and the bloom is pretty continuous for a season.

Seeds planted on a layer of milled sphagnum moss germinate in a few days and the plants are easy to transplant. Pot in a two-and-a-half-incher with Light Mix and place in partial direct light in the window or close to the tubes in the light garden. It's a heavy drinker but requires little fertilizer. Keep the temperature above sixty degrees F. The plant is very subject to mite, which is often carried by the seed itself. The loss of a few leaves is disastrous, for then it has a most naked appearance, not being very leafy to start with. Blooming it is the easiest part of this plant.

Park Seed Company has a *Cuphea* it calls 'Firefly', whose flowers resemble the southern Tar Flower but are a brighter cerise. It has a hairy tube and petals, two of which are larger than the other three. We have not tried this plant, which is described as dwarf and neat, but culture is the same as *C. platycentra* and it should be more satisfactory.

Dipladenia. Apocynaceae. Tropical South America. Beautiful flowering vines for the window.

Buy for bloom in spring
HEIGHT: 2 to 3 feet or more if not
  pruned
COLOR OF BLOOM: pink
HABIT: vine
LIGHT: bright indirect
TEMPERATURE: minimum 65 degrees F.
MOISTURE: moist March to November;
  dryish November to February
TRIMMING: keep cutting back to bush
PROPAGATION: stem cuttings in spring

The big cupped and lobed flowers in gorgeous shades of pink or pure white are so handsome on this vine that one wishes that *Dipladenia* were a little easier to handle. There are three principal species: *D. boliviensis*, with white flowers, and *splendens* and *sanderi* with pink flowers. *Splendens* has big eight-inch leaves and is a pretty rampant vine. Most of the plants offered are simply labeled *Dipladenia rosea* and are probably cultivars of *sanderi*. They can vary considerably as to adaptability.

Usually *Dipladenia* is offered in bloom in eight- or ten-inch pots as an eighteen-inch to two-foot plant. At home it takes off like a shot and does more growing than blooming. If trimmed, it is likely to just sulk. Only if you are lucky will you find a plant that behaves itself. If so, you *can* trim it and it will bloom from short growths. So you have the choice of either growing it all around your window on a trellis—planted eventually in a tub—or taking the chance with pruning and some potbinding to keep it under control. It may work if the plant finds your environment to its liking. Such a beauty is worth a try.

Place it in bright indirect light and keep it at normal house temperature of sixty-five degrees F. or higher with a humidity of fifty percent. Maintain moisture but be careful not to allow any water to stand in the saucer. If potted in ordinary soil by the nursery, repot it in Rich Mix with lime chips when you get it home. Fertilize lightly with every watering. The plant will recover much faster this way and may start to bloom quickly. Duration of bloom is from March or April to November. In winter, keep a bit dryer and repot in February, watering well before making the change. Cuttings root easily in moist vermiculite.

Dipladenia is very subject to spider mites and a No-Pest Strip should be nearby to ward them off. Warmth, high humidity and good light are absolutely necessary to keep this plant flowering.

Epiphyllum hybrids. _Cactaceae._ Central America. Spectacular and easy spring bloomers for the window garden.

Buy for bloom in February–March

HEIGHT PLUS LENGTH OF STEMS: variable; maximum 18 inches high but may trail 6 feet or more

COLOR OF BLOOM: red, white, yellow

HABIT: spreading and hanging

LIGHT: bright indirect; full sun in winter

TEMPERATURE: minimum 50 degrees F. in winter; minimum 65 degrees in summer

MOISTURE: moist February to September–dryish October to March

TRIMMING: cut off excessive lengths any time

PROPAGATION: stem cuttings in spring and summer

The Epiphyllums are epiphytic (growing in trees) cacti, resembling very large Christmas cacti. The stems of some varieties are more upright while others are hanging; and they are rather leaflike in structure in a succulent way. There are no more magnificent flowers than the vividly-colored six- and eight-inch ones which last one, at most two, days. However, plenty of buds are formed and the flowering period lasts for weeks. Epiphyllums have been much hybridized in Germany. Our nurseries sell them unlabeled, and if you want specific named varieties you must buy the plants from specialists.

Grow Epiphyllums in tall pots or baskets. Like most succulents, they prefer a small container. Use Rich Mix with sphagnum instead of peat moss. Fill the bottom of the pot or basket with drainage materials, as good aeration and loose soil is a must.

After flowering in the spring give the plants regular waterings and balanced-formula fertilizer. Fish emulsion is considered best by many growers. Direct sunlight should be avoided but the plants must be set in bright light. In the fall, slow down watering to once a week. The roots should never be absolutely dry but, with the cooler temperatures, never soggy. Amount of watering at any time of year will very much depend on the texture of the soil. If it is very light, you will have to watch closely to avoid drying out the roots.

In winter you can give full sun. Then, when new growth starts, after the turn of the year, resume regular watering and fertilizing until buds and flowers appear in March, April or May. Healthy plants will produce an extraordinary number of these large blossoms.

Pieces of stem, after a few days of drying out, root very readily in moist sand at a temperature of seventy degrees F. or better. By cutting your plants back in the fall you will deprive yourself of their full magnificence but will prevent them from taking over more space than you can afford.

Euphorbia splendens bojeri. Euphorbiaceae. Madagascar. Crown of Thorns. Windowsill or light garden. Everblooming when subjected to daily bright light.

Buy for bloom any time
HEIGHT: pruned to maximum of 12 inches
COLOR OF BLOOM: red
HABIT: shrubby, thorny
LIGHT: full sun or bright indirect
TEMPERATURE: minimum 65 degrees F.
MOISTURE: always wet
TRIMMING: prune branch tips for bushiness
PROPAGATION: stem cuttings any time

Euphorbia bojeri is a smaller plant overall than the standard Crown of Thorns and therefore much easier to handle in the house. Like Poinsettias, Crown of Thorns has very small flowers but the surrounding bracts are brilliantly colored and seem to be petals. Those of this *Euphorbia* are kidney-shaped, two in number, opposite each other and brick red. Each peduncle (flowering stem) bears two flowers.

It is one of the miracles of modern growing that a plant living in near-desert conditions in nature, and seasonal in bloom, will flower all the time in the house as long as it has bright light every day and is wet all the time. Our plants sometimes stand in water for days. And very few plants can look as attractive as this one with its thick branches, its spines, its soft green foliage and plenty of bright flowers.

In one other respect it does not behave like a desert plant. Our Light Mix or even Rich Mix, with lime added, suits it perfectly. It will grow in house temperatures from fifty-five degrees F. up and humidity requirements are low. Once it gets going, it causes no trouble at all. That is why you will find it at variety stores—one of the few they carry which really blooms.

Given the chance, *bojeri* can grow into a pretty big shrub for the house. There is really nothing to prevent it becoming a three- or four-footer given a sufficiently large pot. However, it takes kindly to trimming and can be trained a maximum of a foot high and across by persistent pruning. The cuttings becomes new plants, of course, if set in a propagating box. The spines are sharp—watch out. You have also never seen any plant "bleed" like this one does. To stanch the flow of white sap when you cut off a branch light a match and apply heat to end of the cutting for a moment. The cuttings root in about three weeks, but you must be careful not to allow the vermiculite to become overmoist and to see that the plants have good light. Then they are as easy as any others and will bloom when they are only a couple of inches high.

Some growers have selected especially large flowering plants such as the hybrid *Euphorbia* 'Keysii', with larger and more numerous flowers per peduncle. It is most attractive, though not as regular a bloomer. This is also true of other full-size varieties of *Euphorbia splendens* or its hybrids, which come in a number of shades from pink to red, and even in yellow. Of them all *bojeri* is the only foolproof one.

Exacum affine. Gentianaceae. Socotra. Biennial. Everblooming for a season or up to a year on windowsill or under artificial light. Good terrarium plant under artificial light.

Buy for bloom at any time
HEIGHT: 3–6 inches, to one foot
COLOR OF BLOOM: blue
HABIT: fleshy, bushy
LIGHT: partial sun
TEMPERATURE: minimum 65 degrees F.
MOISTURE: just moist at all times
TRIMMING: nip off dead flowers and
   part of stem to encourage bushing
PROPAGATION: seed or stem cuttings

No other plant we know flowers blue so compactly and in such profusion as *Exacum*. It is a truly easy plant in the house and doesn't even attract pests. In fact its only drawback is that the flowers are so numerous that their remains must be promptly removed to make room for the next crop. And so rapidly does this take place, despite the fact that individual flowers last for several days, that it requires constant grooming.

Exacum affine grows up to a foot high, but usually much less—it is not a stretching plant. The leaves are closely packed, fleshy, short-stemmed and bright green. Thus it forms a tight round mound of greenery. The flowers consist of five rounded petals with a cluster of deep yellow stamens pouring down from the throat. In addition to the blue there is a white variety and a dwarf introduction which we have found less satisfactory and shorter-lived.

Grow the plants from seed which is available from any number of seedsmen and sow in late summer or early fall for all-winter bloom. The seed requires light to germinate and takes about fifteen days. When you have plants, you can also grow more from cuttings which are a little balky but usually come through in about three weeks in a propagating box containing moist vermiculite.

The new plants will start to bloom when only a couple of inches high in the window or under lights. They use Rich Mix, with moderate

fertilizing and moisture without sogginess. But keep them at sixty degrees
F. and over, or they can become mildewed or suffer from stem rot.

Fuchsia triphylla. Onagraceae.   West Indies. A rather difficult summer-
blooming house plant that does best under artificial light.

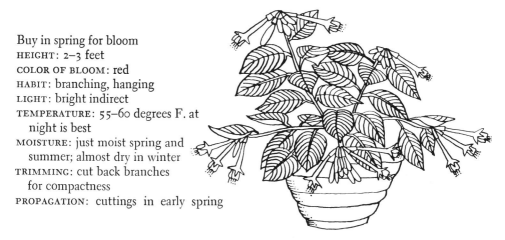

Buy in spring for bloom
HEIGHT: 2–3 feet
COLOR OF BLOOM: red
HABIT: branching, hanging
LIGHT: bright indirect
TEMPERATURE: 55–60 degrees F. at
   night is best
MOISTURE: just moist spring and
   summer; almost dry in winter
TRIMMING: cut back branches
   for compactness
PROPAGATION: cuttings in early spring

We find it more difficult to write about the older blooming house plants.
They made do but were never really satisfactory. A good deal of expertise
was required to keep them healthy and blooming. Fuchsias are so much
better hanging in a basket on the porch for they require cool nights and
plenty of clean air and humidity. Out of doors they benefit from dew at
night. No plant draws more white flies than this one, and they seem to
come from the ends of the earth to find it. On the other hand, Fuchsias
are very beautiful plants and we should make the attempt to grow them
indoors. Perhaps the hybridizers will favor us by someday producing
more adaptable plants.

   Most people are familiar with Fuchsias of the petticoat varieties.
But another kind, equally beautiful in our eyes, does have some merit
as a house plant. These are the *F. triphylla* hybrids and an old variety
called 'Gartenmeister Bonstedt' which originally was either a selection or
hybrid. These plants have green leaves, deep purple beneath and one-and-
a-half-inch tube flowers flaring into triangular lobes. The color ranges from
red through orange-red to near pink. Though they are less showy
individually than those of the petticoat hybrids the flowers are produced

in such number as linear clusters that a well-grown plant can be very beautiful.

F. triphylla does not have as many growths from the soil as others and its stems are somewhat woodier, though the branches arch. At least it does not need a basket and will do quite well in a five-inch pot. Given the chance, these plants can grow two or three feet high in a larger pot and make magnificent specimen plants simply dripping with flowers. But for most people and most homes they should be kept within bounds by pruning.

Buy a *triphylla hybrid* in the spring as a small plant and, as soon as you have it home, remove all flowers and buds. Get rid of the dirt in which it is potted by washing carefully in lukewarm water, and repot in Rich Mix in a five- or six-inch plastic pot. Spray or wash all the leaves to remove the eggs of white flies.

Put the plant in an east window or at the side of a south or west window. Under lights, you can set it initially six inches away and near the center, later gradually moving it to the side. It will be very happy to have air-conditioning and, lacking that, good ventilation from open windows. Mist it every morning.

Keep the soil moist, not wet, and fertilize regularly with a balanced solution (20–20–20, for instance). In the house you will have to trim back weak stems and remove dead flowers to keep it neat.

Now comes the rub. In the fall you can discard your *Fuchsia* or try to carry it over the winter. It's rather cranky about the latter. In September, gradually withdraw water until all the leaves drop off. Keep the pot almost dry, watering very lightly every two weeks. The difficulty is that it likes fifty degree F. temperatures at this time, and, if it is warmer, the soil dries out more rapidly so that the watering period is hard to judge. On the other hand, if it receives excess water *plus* warmth it will green up prematurely.

In February repot the plant in new soil, and trim back the stems— using the cuttings for propagation—and gradually increase moisture. If lucky, you will be back in business. We prefer to use the plants developed from the cuttings and discard the old one.

In the house Fuchsias are very subject to leaf drop. If this has been caused by white fly it is easy to diagnose. Shake the plant and snow will fly upward. In this case we usually stand three feet away and give it a blast of House and Garden Raid. Then we give the plant repeated washings on successive days. Another cause of leaf drop is fungal infection. Benlate spray should take care of it.

Gardenia jasminoides. Rubiaceae. China. Gardenia.

Buy in spring for bloom
HEIGHT: to 2 feet in the house
COLOR OF BLOOM: white
HABIT: bushy
LIGHT: partial shade
TEMPERATURE: during bud formation
    60–65 degrees F.; summer 65 degrees
    F. minimum
MOISTURE: very wet except just moist in
    midwinter
TRIMMING: keep well pruned after
    blooming
PROPAGATION: cuttings from young
    wood

Alas, Gardenias! How many people love them for their white flowers and their rich perfume and buy them in the spring loaded with buds only to watch every bud turn brown and the plant begin to droop. This is another oldster in the house plant category which gives trouble. Success is usually the result of two factors: a "Gardenia thumb" and a good plant. Nursery-grown stock varies in quality. If you find a plant which performs for you treasure it.

We don't claim that our own method is foolproof, and it involves some anguish. So we don't know whether you will want to try it. However, one has to have some method, and this is ours.

When you bring your plant home, ruthlessly cut off all buds and trim the plant to a compact shape. We do this because we find that usually the shock of moving the plant to a new environment is more than it can take and still make the effort to bloom. Keep the plant moist and do not fertilize. Place it in reflected sunlight or at either end of the light garden. Keep it warm—over sixty-five degrees F. at all times.

After one month in these conditions, remove the plant from its pot and wash off old soil with lukewarm water. Replant in Rich Mix without lime and with a tablespoon of Sequestrene (chelated iron plus trace elements) added. Firm the soil very carefully around the roots so that there will be no air holes. Give the plant another two or three weeks of rest as above. Remove any buds that have formed during this period.

Now set it in an east window, or bright reflected light, or one foot below the tubes. Keep moist but not soggy. Never allow it to dry out even for a day. Spray the leaves with water daily and maintain high humidity. After a couple of weeks, if it is doing well, start fertilizing weekly with high nitrate formula.

About the middle of September water the plant more thoroughly and let it stand in water in its saucer. Be sure to continue to keep it warm and move it to a more lighted position as the sun is no longer so intense and the days are shorter. If buds appear, remove every other one at first.

If the plant likes you it will bloom and you can now let it run as it pleases, easing up on the water in midwinter. In spring cut it back again and let it rest through the summer. You may have to move it to a bigger pot. In fact, repotting in fresh soil will do it good.

Young wood will root in moist vermiculite at a temperature of sixty-five to seventy degrees F.

Good growing!

Miniature Geraniums (*Pelargoniums*). *Geraniaceae*. South Africa. Complex hybrids. Perennial plants usually treated as annuals for light garden and window.

Buy for bloom in January or February
HEIGHT: miniatures to 3 inches; dwarfs
   6 to 8 inches
COLOR OF BLOOM: red, white, pink,
   orange
HABIT: compact-branched
LIGHT: very bright
TEMPERATURE: consistently cool; maxi-
   mum 75 degrees F.
TRIMMING: prune to shape
PROPAGATION: stem cuttings at 70
   degrees F.

If you wish, you can grow the large outdoor Geraniums in the light garden in winter, which is a challenge that has tempted many an amateur lately. Inherently, however, these are not proper house plants. In our opinion, they are too big and much too coarse. Out of doors, in solid beds, they serve an ornamental purpose, and finely grown plants may look great in pots, but they are never really happy in the house.

Miniature and dwarf Geraniums are another matter. The miniatures are two to three inches high and the dwarfs may grow to six or eight inches. Heads are looser and fewer-flowered, but the individual blossoms show much greater variation of form and coloring. We know few plants more exquisite than these when well grown. Their cultivation can become a true cult for they have an endless fascination. Why, then, are they not more popular?

How one of our friends grows them to perfection tells us why. He built a large cabinet much like an old icebox with glass doors at the top and a storage area in the bottom. In the upper part he had two shelves of fluorescent tubes. The Geraniums were in trays below each set of lights. The bottom contained an air-conditioner which kept the temperature at fifty-five to sixty-five degrees F.

The answer is that these Geraniums are too cool-growing for most homes. They will do fine in well-ventilated sun porches in the northern states or in country houses where cool temperatures are maintained. Without this condition the plants will bloom for a while but gradually lose their vigor and succumb to fungal diseases.

The other requirements are simple enough. They like good light—a sunny window or a position under the center of the lights—a chance to dry out between waterings, fertilizers once a week and a Light Mix or sand with humus. When properly grown they will bloom continuously. And on these plants a single fine flower at a time makes a brave show, but each peduncle bears a number of them.

Cuttings of the younger growth root easily in moist vermiculite or sand, with the propagating box only partly closed, as excess humidity is not appreciated.

As the plants grow older they can assume the aspect of a bonsai. We had a 'Variegated Kleiner Liebling' in a Japanese pot which looked for all the world like a finely trained succulent or a little twisted tree. It is difficult to exaggerate the charm of these plants. An easy one is 'Salmon

Comet'. 'Sneezy', a semidwarf, has marvelous red-and-white flowers. Petals take many forms from narrow to round, and there are doubles too. There are dozens of fine forms with names like 'Prince Valiant', 'Dopey' (there is a whole Snow White dwarf series), 'Tiny Tim', planet names like 'Saturn' and 'Jupiter' and an old one, 'Mme. Fournier'. So even the names are interesting.

If you can find the right plant "furniture" to provide optimum conditions, as our friend did, you should enjoy converting it to a Geranium nursery.

GESNERIADS

One of the strangest reactions one comes across these days among amateur indoor growers is a closed mind against the name gesneriad, as if it were too difficult to remember. Let us explain that these are members of the family *Gesneriaceae*, whose most popular members for a long time have been the Gloxinias and African Violets. The African Violet has spawned a cult and everybody is rather overwhelmed by the volume of novelties constantly developed in its genus, *Saintpaulia*. But the objection is largely capricious as the other gesneriads form an excessively large proportion of all the best house plants. But just a few families have always contributed many more good indoor plants than the others. We can mention the Begonias, the orchids, the bromeliads and the *Acanthus* family. Anyone who is familiar with the range of the gesneriads must agree that the variety of colorings and forms can hardly be matched anywhere in the plant world except among the orchids. The contrasts are really astonishing. There are such tiny flowers as *Sinningia pusilla* and such large ones as the Gloxinias and *Streptocarpus*. Every color is represented by many shades and textures.

But the real advantage of the gesneriads is their adaptability to home culture. By and large, they are compact, require relatively little light to bloom, and will tolerate house temperatures. Furthermore, they can be easily multiplied. Recent hybridizing indicates that few families are capable of as much manipulation as to form and color as this one. Finally, no other family contributes so many plants which are, in the true sense, everblooming. Most of them can be grown on the windowsill and under lights, and some are ideal for terrariums. Grow gesneriads and you will love them.

Achimenes. Gesneriaceae. Central America. Spring- and summer-blooming in many colors. Does well in country windows and light gardens but is very sensitive to aerial pollution.

Buy for bloom in March–April
HEIGHT: 3 to 10 inches
COLOR OF BLOOM: blue, pink, white,
   yellow
HABIT: bushy, spreading
LIGHT: partial sun
TEMPERATURE: minimum 65 degrees F.
MOISTURE: evenly moist March–
   September; rhizomes dormant
   September–March
PROPAGATION: by rhizomes

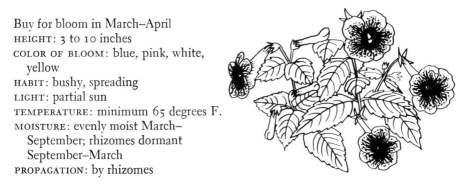

Achimenes is grown principally from scaly rhizomes which are part of the root system and are propagated in quantity during the blooming season. These rhizomes are up to an inch long and a quarter of an inch in diameter, with fleshy scales arranged much like those of a pine cone. In spring growth starts at one tip and then they are planted horizontally just below the surface of the mix. Three can go into a four-inch pot with Rich Mix.

The pots are placed in bright indirect light in the window or close to the tubes, watered regularly, and fed with full-strength balanced fertilizer. Stems should be nipped promptly at the tips and pruning should continue in order to make bushy plants. As soon as the first flower blooms, they can be lowered to a foot from the lights and placed in a somewhat less sunny spot on the windowsill. Throughout spring and summer *Achimenes* will bloom in profusion from the axils of the leaves.

Never allow the pot to dry out. Maintain a minimum temperature of sixty-five degrees F. and humidity of fifty percent or higher. It is most important to give *Achimenes* a quick start and to have it blooming when quite small.

In the fall leaves will start to dry and rhizomes, similar to the ones in the soil, may develop instead of flowers on the branches. These can also be used for propagation but are less reliable than the others. Dry out the soil and knock the plant out of the pot. Mixed with the regular roots you will find clusters of rhizomes. Separate these carefully—they are very brittle. Broken pieces will grow but are less vigorous. Store the rhizomes with labels in plastic bags until the following spring.

We would like very much to bloom *Achimenes* in winter. It is possible if the plants are dried out and the rhizomes stored in June or July that they will sprout in October or November. A. 'Pulchella, Jr.' appears to be most amenable to this treatment.

The flowers have tubes with broadly flared, shallow-lobed openings. All the colors of the spectrum seem to be represented, plus beautiful markings and veinings. The size of the plants varies from a six-inch spread to two feet, and the flowers from one inch to two and a half inches. The great color variety is due to more than a century of breeding.

It is most unfortunate that they will not tolerate city conditions. In all probability aerial pollution is the cause. The plants grow well enough and will even set buds, but the flowers refuse to open. We are constantly on the lookout for some hybrid or mutation which will bloom in a city apartment. A. 'Tarantella' from Geo. W. Park Seed Company (Michelssen hybrids) may do the trick. It is an exquisite dwarf, easy to grow, with the deepest pink flowers. Two others are 'Menuett', also pink, and 'Valse Bleu', blue with white eye. These are six-inch plants.

Other varieties chosen for general growing from extensive catalog listings are:

'Ambroise Verschaffelt', an old hybrid with purple-veined white flowers
A. *bella*, purple and white, very compact
A. 'Camille Brozzoni', upright with lavender flowers
A. 'Cardinal Velvet' ('Master Ingram'), big red flower, yellow throat
A. 'Early Arnold'
A. *flava*, yellow
A. *heterophylla*, bright orange, yellow throat
A. 'Little Beauty', pink, compact
A. *longiflora*, blue
A. 'Pulchella, Jr.'

A. 'Sparkle' (Kartuz cross), rose-pink

A. 'Wetterlow's Triumph', big pink blossoms

A. 'Yellow Beauty', large yellow

We have not included the late bloomers, preferring the early ones.

Columnea **'Chanticleer'.** *Gesneriaceae.* Central America. Goldfish Plant. Everblooming on the windowsill, in the light garden and the terrarium.

Buy for bloom any time
HEIGHT: length of branches to 12 inches
COLOR OF BLOOM: orange
HABIT: spreading, trailing
LIGHT: partial shade
TEMPERATURE: minimum 65 degrees F.
MOISTURE: evenly moist
TRIMMING: cut back lengthy branches
PROPAGATION: stem cuttings

The house plant repertory has been immeasurably enriched by the introduction of species Columneas only a few years ago, and their hybridization. The flowers, orange, red, yellow or pink, are sometimes as long as four inches and each one may last for weeks. The shape is that of a fish, with a tubular body, a broad upper lobe of a head flanked by fins, and a shorter curled lower lobe. The fruits are a large white berry.

Over a number of years important progress was made at Cornell University in the hybridization of showier plants. Since then the effort has been directed more to increasing the everblooming qualities—with notable success. Many of the best of the original Columneas were purely hanging plants with long, lax streamers. Now there are many hybrids with strong branches and a more horizontal or erect habit which is far better suited to the needs of the indoor grower. There are now so many new plants being marketed that it is difficult to tell some of them apart, or to find the time to test them all. But an increasing number are easy to grow and bloom continuously.

Our choice here is simply the hybrid we consider the easiest to handle and the most reliable, although it is far from being the most spectacular. The flower is a soft orange and about an inch and a half long at best. It has sturdy but not too heavy branches, trims back well and can be trained, and it blooms with little provocation all year round. It is also sufficiently small to fit, with occasional trimming, into a terrarium, where it makes a most impressive show.

The light requirement of all Columneas is usually rather low; they like a situation which is out of direct sunlight but where there is a good bright glow. In a greenhouse, hung in baskets, they are symmetrical and, if they are large trailers, hang to floor level yet bloom all the way down to the very tips. In a light garden they grow toward the strongest light. Even the most upright types must be *hung* below the tubes. We use short wire hook hangers and suspend the pots from the top of the fixture or the crack separating its two parts. Flowers bloom quite close to the tubes and the trailing branches which hang down, perhaps as much as eighteen inches, do just as well. Yet we have found that it is hard to bloom them (at least in the city) unless the top of the plant is well lighted. This may be a fallacy but so far in practice that is what works.

On a sun porch or in a window they should also be suspended but will do best if they are not subjected to direct sun for more than an hour or two daily. On the other hand, they do require brightness for at least five hours and, if there is a cloudy spell, only green growth will be produced.

'Chanticleer', at least, does not mind being moist all the time. Those Columneas which are more seasonal in bloom and growth must be kept rather dry during their period(s) of resting. We find that many of them bloom best when allowed also to dry out a bit between light moistenings. Various species and cultivars are different in this respect. But 'Chanticleer' is not temperamental and just blooms away.

Pot all Columneas rather loosely in Rich Mix with plenty of lime, and fertilize with balanced formula at every watering. We use rather small pots for these spreading plants. A three-incher will do very well, and it may be that they like a bit of potbinding. When buds form we usually switch to high phosphate-potash fertilizers. So far none of our Columneas have been infested by insects but if mite does attack them, the No-Pest Strip will get rid of them.

In the house a most important part of growing Columneas is trimming. The upright types, which are preferable to the trailers, still have a more horizontal growth, though when the stems are long enough they will hang down. The only difference is that they are thick and stiff instead of being stringy. Also, these thicker stems will branch freely if the tips are nipped back. So nipping should be done regularly. Instead of long streamers covered with flowers you will have a many-branched plant doing the same thing. In the house, this is far more desirable.

Temperatures should be over sixty-five degrees F. for bloom, the humidity fifty percent or better—and the plants are helped by frequent misting. Cold water will discolor the leaves. They prefer watering from the top.

What else can we say? In spite of all, Columneas present difficulties for some growers and we cannot say we know the cause. For others they bloom like crazy and are impressively beautiful.

Columnea erythrophaea. Gesneriaceae.   Central America.

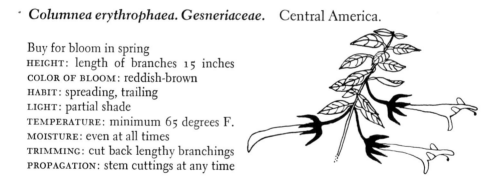

Buy for bloom in spring
HEIGHT: length of branches 15 inches
COLOR OF BLOOM: reddish-brown
HABIT: spreading, trailing
LIGHT: partial shade
TEMPERATURE: minimum 65 degrees F.
MOISTURE: even at all times
TRIMMING: cut back lengthy branchings
PROPAGATION: stem cuttings at any time

This combination of vowels in the species will be a stumbling block to some, so here is the way it is pronounced—airithropheea—accent on next to last syllable.

It is a newly introduced species which is likely to start a whole new trend in Columneas. The distinguishing feature is a long pedicel, or stem, to the flower. Most Columneas have very short ones. Also, *erythrophaea* has a big, attractive, pleated calyx. The flower is very long—three inches or more—and rather narrow; and, because of the pedicel, it hangs well free of the branches, which are fairly thick and grow horizontally. The color is reddish-brown, but a new, unnamed clone is brilliant orange.

This is a spectacular plant in bloom, which, provided conditions are right, is an all year rounder.

Cultural directions are the same as for *C.* 'Chanticleer'. *Erythrophaea* looks particularly well arranged in a pot as a series of well-rooted cuttings and with each single stem cutting no more than eight inches long. The effect of the suspended flowers is magnificent.

Other Columneas with everblooming tendency are: *C.* 'Early Bird', *C.* 'Yellow Dragon' and *C.* 'Yellow Gold'. New varieties are appearing rapidly, and your nurseryman should be consulted for plants with best vigor and bloom.

Episcia **'Cygnet'.** *Gesneriaceae.* Central America. Hybrid for pot or basket in window or under lights. Everblooming. Juveniles can be grown in terrariums.

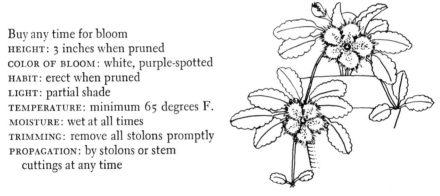

Buy any time for bloom
HEIGHT: 3 inches when pruned
COLOR OF BLOOM: white, purple-spotted
HABIT: erect when pruned
LIGHT: partial shade
TEMPERATURE: minimum 65 degrees F.
MOISTURE: wet at all times
TRIMMING: remove all stolons promptly
PROPAGATION: by stolons or stem
    cuttings at any time

When we saw 'Cygnet' for the first time it was growing in a basket and hanging down in a rather disorderly way. But the flowers were pretty and larger than other Episcias. The nurseryman disparaged it as having a poor habit. We bought it, nevertheless, and over the years have learned to handle it so that it remains as neat as you could wish and never stops blooming. In our opinion it is the easiest to grow and train of all the Episcias. The only objection is that the foliage is rather plain.

The flower is over an inch across, white, beautifully fringed, the throat dotted with purple. Flowers last two or three days at most but the production of bloom per inch of stem over a long period is tremendous.

Episcia 'Cygnet' is a hybrid of two white-flowered species which are not at all easy to bloom. It has hairy gray-green foliage, scalloped along the edges and tapering to a long petiole. The cause of its bad habit is the production of quantities of stolons (suckers), which, if allowed to grow, extend like ropes down the side of pot or basket and produce rosettes and flowers at the tips. All Episcias have this tendency, but in some at least the center stem is thick and sturdy.

'Cygnet' requires special training for flower production.

Since this *Episcia* is sterile, you must start with a plant. Pot it up in Rich Mix and keep very moist at all times. It is more tolerant of real wetness than other Episcias. Feed regularly with balanced fertilizer. In the city window it requires an east or west situation; in the country it will do well with reflected light. Flowering will depend on the number of successive cloudy days. But placed four or five inches below fluorescent tubes and given a sixteen-hour day, it will bloom continuously. High humidity is beneficial but not a requirement. The temperature should always be above sixty-five degrees F. Ours have never been bothered by pests.

As the plant grows, snip off all stolons at the base. The tips with their leafy rosettes can be propagated in moist vermiculite. While the plant is still small—no more than two inches high—you will have months of bloom, with two flowers at a time that are really outsize in proportion. Gradually it will outgrow the pot, and in larger quarters will put up more rosettes. Keep trimming those stolons. After a goodly while you may have a five- or six-inch pot mounded with stems and leaves no more than three inches high and all blooming. Single stems can then be removed for very rapid propagation and quick blooming. In this way, your plant will always be neat and flowering.

E. 'Cygnet' makes a splendid terrarium plant using the single stems in two-inch pots.

This is an outstanding example of the way we can train plants according to our needs. Of course the plant itself must be amenable, and 'Cygnet' is very obliging. It's a treasure.

Episcia 'Moss Agate'. *Gesneriaceae.* Central America. The most ever-blooming and one of the most attractive of the ornamental-leaved Episcias. Windowsill or light garden.

Buy for best bloom in spring
HEIGHT: to 10 inches but will trail 12
    inches
COLOR OF BLOOM: tomato red
HABIT: naturally trailing
LIGHT: bright indirect
TEMPERATURE: minimum 65 degrees F.
MOISTURE: evenly moist
TRIMMING: remove stolons; support stem
PROPAGATION: stem or stolon cuttings

The habit of the great majority of Episcias has all the disadvantages of E. 'Cygnet' except that the hybrids derived from other species have far more beautiful leaves. These range from two to six inches in length and are roughly oval. Because of their size and shape, the trailing stems do not look naked as with 'Cygnet' but, on the contrary, form beautiful masses of overlapping foliage.

The wonderful leaves are quilted and veined, the veining breaking up areas of brown or green, plain or in combination with silver. Two most unusual plants, E. 'Cleopatra' and E. 'Ember Lace', are zoned in white, pink and green, making a display which is one of the most spectacular in the whole plant kingdom.

The flowers are not over an inch in length and are wide-lobed. The majority are in shades of orange to deep tomato red. A few are pink. 'Moss Agate' has large, beautifully quilted leaves and brilliant tomato-red flowers which are somewhat fringed and exquisitely frosted in the throat. It is an easy, sturdy and handsome plant and a most reliable bloomer on windowsill, in light garden, in the city and in the country.

Grown in the greenhouse in a large basket, these Episcias form symmetrical masses of foliage dotted with bright flowers. In the house, such huge plants are out of the question. We have the choice of supporting Episcia in pots so that a small plant can trail or developing the single thick but rather weak central stem, at first by removing all stolons, and later by tying the stem to a short stake.

In a normal pot the stolons become both an interference with the growth of the plant and distinctly untidy. For this reason we cut them all off, use them for the propagation of new plants, and grow the single stem as long as it continues to be presentable.

Start young Episcias in one-and-a-half to two-inch pots with Rich Mix. They need very good bright light but not direct sun; place them four inches below the tubes. They respond well to plenty of lime in the mix. Watering is a little tricky. They just do not like sogginess and are subject to crown rot. Water when the soil is dryish. A temperature of sixty-five degrees F. or better and humidity of fifty percent benefits these plants. Frequent misting of the leaves prevents curling and encourages bloom. Fertilize with high phosphate-potash regularly. The plant rarely reaches a height of more than eight inches even with support of the stem. Be particularly sparing of water during cool periods in the winter.

Other good flowering Episcias are *E.* 'Acajou', one of the original cultivars, *E.* 'Silver Sheen', a larger-leaved improved form, and *E.* 'Shimmer'.

Gesneria cuneifolia. Gesneriaceae.   West Indies. Window. Light garden. Terrarium. Everblooming.

Buy for bloom any time
HEIGHT: 2–3 inches
COLOR OF BLOOM: red
HABIT: low rosette
LIGHT: partial shade
TEMPERATURE: minimum 65 degrees F.
MOISTURE: very wet at all times
PROPAGATION: seed

Gesneria cuneifolia is among the most desirable small plants for the house. For sheer floriferousness it has no competition whatsoever. We have had a *Gesneria cuneifolia* 'Quebradillas' in a six-inch pot blooming with a minimum of thirty flowers a day for a solid year with hardly any noticeable growth of the plant. It has the reputation of being purely a terrarium plant, but will grow outside a terrarium in moderate humidity of forty percent or more. The only serious problem is its initial slow growth from seed or cutting. For this reason the average amateur is advised to acquire plants from a nursery.

The flowers are inch-long, narrow tubes flaring into five short lobes. The plant appears stemless at first but gradually the whorls of long shiny spatulate leaves start moving upward and a short stem appears. A well-grown *Gesneria cuneifolia* may have a large number of these single stems, but the plant as a whole will be a rounded mound of overlapping leaves with flowers in great numbers peeking out from under or standing above the foliage.

There are three different forms of this plant. *G. cuneifolia* has red flowers; the form 'El Yunque' is longitudinally half burnt orange and half red; and 'Quebradillas' has yellow flowers with an orange tip. 'Quebradillas' we consider the best of the three because the flower stems are longer and the flowers held well above the foliage. These plants are fertile. In addition, there is a nonfertile cross between *G. citrina* and *G. cuneifolia* called 'Lemon Drop' which has true golden-yellow flowers and is incredibly floriferous. As it grows, the stem looks like a porcupine, so thick are the new and old flower stems, in addition to all those growing out of the top of the plant. Kartuz Nurseries is propagating this plant.

There are two absolute requirements for *Gesneria*. Temperature should not drop below sixty-five degrees F.—danger of rot begins at sixty degrees F. It must be wet at all times. Even a day of dryness will kill it.

Otherwise it can be treated as one of the crowd. In the window, give partial light—no direct sun (except for short periods in the city). Under lights, it can be ten inches below the source. Flowering is not guaranteed in a window if there are many days of cloudy weather. As a terrarium plant *Gesneria* is ideal, blooming as far as eighteen inches from the lights and luxuriating in the humidity. Its lowness (maximum height about five inches) and compact habit are very desirable. Any mild fertilizer solution seems to agree with it.

Gesneria often self-pollinates and sets seed which is tiny but viable. Plants germinate in a week or ten days and can be transplanted a couple of weeks later (with the help of a hand lens). Keep them in a propagation box until they are large enough (about an inch across) to transplant to two-inch pots. Four inches is the maximum required except for a monster plant. Occasionally you will have enough stems and rosettes on large plants to cut these free and plant them in your vermiculite propagation box. They may do well, but we have generally found that they don't and that we are safer using seed.

Nematanthus (formerly *Hypocyrta*). *Gesneriaceae.* Tropical America. Candy Corn Plant. Intermittent bloomers for window or light garden.

Buy for bloom in the spring
HEIGHT: erect types to 10 inches;
    trailing branches to 2 feet or more
COLOR OF BLOOM: orange
HABIT: some erect, some trailing and
    spreading
LIGHT: bright indirect
TEMPERATURE: minimum 60 degrees F.
MOISTURE: evenly moist
TRIMMING: prune drastically for com-
    pactness
PROPAGATION: stem cuttings

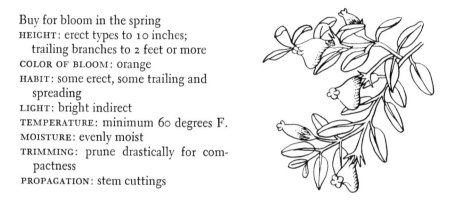

The flower of a Nematanthus is so unusual that, at first sight, a viewer is likely to suspect a joke. It is a tube with a deep keel or pouch, at the end of which is a little opening with minute lobes. The color may be bright orange, plain or tipped with yellow, or a most unusual horizontal striping of orange and chestnut. The contrast with the shiny, waxy foliage is very striking.

How quickly the indoor plant world is changing is demonstrated by the history of *Nematanthus.* In 1957 Dr. Harold E. Moore, Jr., a major authority, wrote *African Violets, Gloxinias and Their Relatives* and included only the species called at that time *Hypocyrta nummularia.* We remember trying to grow this pretty plant. It is a trailer with hairy small opposite leaves and delightful pouch flowers, bright vermillion with a violet band around the neck of the opening and yellow lobes. Mrs. Frances N. Batcheller described it as "like a red bag tied with a black ribbon." It is a charmer but tough to grow, for it is excessively temperamental, has periods of semidormancy and is the devil to water properly.

Then came *N. wettsteinii,* a tremendous improvement. It has incredibly shiny deep green oval leaves on thin, hanging branches—like strings of finest jade. The pouched flowers are orange tipped, turning yellow at the opening. That is why it came to be called the Candy Corn plant. It makes a wonderful small pot plant in the window or under the lights, but can also be grown in big baskets with masses of green tumbling down lighted up by numerous flowers. Although it blooms best in the spring, it can be made to flower by good culture most of the year.

Around the same time a number of other jungle imports arrived and were cultivated. Best of these was N. *radicans*, a larger-leaved and thicker-stemmed plant with orange flowers. It was a joy for the nursery as it propagated very easily; but it still is not a very good house plant. The others were tricky plants grown only by enthusiasts.

In 1969 William Saylor, of Brewster, Massachusetts, systematically crossed most of the Nematanthus in cultivation and came up with some interesting results. One of the hybrids, N. 'Tropicana' (N. *periantho-mega* x N. *radicans*), is a vigorous plant perhaps easier to bloom than N. *wettsteinii*. The leaves are an inch long, of heavy texture and red beneath. The stems are also deep burgundy. The flowers are golden yellow heavily striped with chestnut. Another is N. 'Rio', upright, with hairy, bright orange flowers and green leaves. N. 'Mardi Gras', of still more recent date, produces many more flowers in the axils than 'Tropicana', is more upright but has nearly the same coloration. Experience will tell whether these are lasting introductions. But we can be pretty sure that Nematanthus are here to stay, for they are a fascinating addition to our repertory of house plants.

In case you are confused about the habit of these plants we are describing them individually below:

N. *wettsteinii*—trailing, hanging growth; twiggy when cut back

N. 'Tropicana'—trailing plant, larger overall than N. *wettsteinii*

N. 'Rio'—erect plant with fleshy stems that have a tendency to become leggy if not close to good light

N. 'Mardi Gras', an upright version of 'Tropicana' but shorter stemmed. Rest after each blooming, withholding water

We pot these Nematanthus in Rich Mix and hang those with trailing stems below the tubes. In the window they can be started in a little basket and moved to a larger one later on. The soil should not be packed tight around the roots, since a good deal of aeration is desirable. In the window some direct sun is necessary. Maintain temperatures constantly above sixty degrees F. We find even that a bit trying on the plants; sixty-five degrees F. is better. Because of the loose potting, watering must be almost daily unless there is a cloudy spell.

N. 'Rio' and 'Mardi Gras' tolerate drier conditions than N. 'Tropicana' and N. *wettsteinii*. The upright varieties require trimming more than N. *wettsteinii*. High humidity helps these plants, and they should be misted often. Fertilize regularly.

After a spate of blooming, Nematanthus seem to need some rest. This is particularly true in winter. We are not sure whether this is a consequence of lower temperature in our growing room or a seasonal manifestation. However, once bloom has ceased, for whatever reason, watering should be reduced and no fertilizer used. As we've urged before, never force water or fertilizer on a plant. It will indicate by growth and its consumption of the water whether it is active or resting. If over-watered, leaves will drop and rot may set in. It may be, at least for N. *wettsteinii* and N. 'Tropicana', that if the temperature is maintained constantly over sixty-five degrees with high humidity, growth and bloom can be continuous. These are relatively new plants and very little has been written about their culture. What has is certainly not definitive. We hope our suggestions will help.

Saintpaulia. Gesneriaceae. South Africa. African Violet.

Buy for bloom at any time
HEIGHT: to 4 inches
COLOR OF BLOOM: pink, blue, white,
   purple
HABIT: spreading rosette
LIGHT: partial sun
TEMPERATURE: minimum 65 degrees F.
MOISTURE: evenly moist
PROPAGATION: leaf cuttings

The "miracle plant" of all modern house plants is too familiar to need description. Enormously, permanently and deservedly popular, it has had a strange history—a warning that the golden mean applies also to the culture of plants.

Discovered in 1892 in southern Africa, in moist, shaded locations, it originally had rather insignificant bluish flowers. The various species were found to be particularly adaptable to indoor conditions of low light and to be nearly everblooming. They were easy to hybridize and were very amenable to improvement. About 1938, A.V.'s (for short) started to become popular in this country at almost the same time that the first fluorescent tubes were marketed. The marriage of the two was a perfect one. The plants throve, and light gardening became a reality.

Because it was a compact plant which everybody could afford and which gave endless pleasure, the culture of African Violets spread phenomenally. And as hybridization and selection could be carried on by any amateur, the development of new forms occurred with a frequency probably never attained before with any other plant. The total effect of all this activity was undoubtedly a continuous improvement in floriferousness, flower form and color.

In principle, therefore, all this interest was a good thing; but a good thing can be overdone. Doting A.V. specialists hungered for novelty. And year after year hundreds of new plants were dumped on the market. (The list of one nursery runs annually to fourteen letter-size pages.) The slightest variation in color or leaf was given a name and marketed immediately. Grotesque, tasteless and unnatural distortions were greeted with acclaim. The A.V. became the refuge of the horticulturally ignorant and lost its appeal for those who were more selective. No attempt was made to preserve plants of real merit; these were simply drowned in the next flood of novelties. It is no wonder that a would-be purchaser is dismayed by a whole greenhouse full of different hybrids, of which the vast majority are inferior. How could one identify the better plants? Overall quality also suffered.

On the other hand, sheer surfeit and continuous activity have recently led to the development of some new forms—the miniature and trailing types. At the present rate, they too will soon be contaminated by the novelty craze. It would be most useful if the African Violet societies would make an attempt to select and perpetuate plants of proved merit. Whatever the specialists may like from one week to an-other, the general public needs plants on which it can rely for vigorous growth and bloom.

We cannot recommend any particular named African Violet. Our own choices have been picked up here and there. Some have been discarded after a while; a few keep going and prove their worth. By now we have long lost the original names, or the plants are no longer available. One new extraordinarily perfect grower is Fischer's 'Lisa' from the Ballet series. This plant may serve as an example of what we are looking for in African Violets.

Judging rules set the standards for their appearance. For a long time they were supposed to be cartwheels of symmetrical leaves with a big bunch of bloom in the exact center. Plants were displayed at one time which were two or more feet in diameter—monstrosities which soon lost their popularity. Plants with two leads were definitely taboo. This straitjacket couldn't last forever, and now we have miniature plants and trailers which have broken the spell. A recent acquisition called 'Pique Pixie' blooms for us with a big tuft of nearly upright leaves and soft pink flowers studding the top. Maybe African Violets are being liberated.

Although among the easier plants to grow and bloom in the house, the average A.V. you are likely to buy can be pretty disappointing. Adaptability has by no means kept pace with diversity and there are many complaints of difficulty with the plants. Greenhouse-grown and forced, they all look perfect, but after a month in the home, they stop blooming, leaves shrink in size, and you may have a plant which is rather inferior to some of our other recommendations.

The culture of African Violets is quite simple and the better varieties should perform well. Pot them in Rich Mix with lime, allow to dry out somewhat between waterings (they should never be water-logged) and fertilize with a high phosphate-potash solution. Give them fifty percent or better humidity if possible (this is not vital) or mist their leaves. Set them in a sunny window in the city or partial sun in the country, and eight to fifteen inches under lights. Use room-temperature water and don't drop cold water on the leaves. We water from the bottom.

Large, growing African Violets soon become potbound. They also develop an unsightly stem if of the single rosette type. When this happens you can chop off some of its root and plant deeper in another pot so that the rosette is level with the ground. But we have often found that the plant is never quite the same again. Thus the longevity of the majority of these plants is not that great—certainly not more than a year in good shape.

In fact, all the violets need a considerable amount of grooming and attention. Many of the plants in this list can be allowed to grow as they please but there is always something to do for an A.V. It is not one which can be neglected successfully.

Far better than replanting stemmed plants is to start new ones by means of leaf cuttings with about one-half inch of stem planted in moist vermiculite. The little new growths should be separated and potted up, then nursed into big ones so that you have a constant series of young, vigorous bloomers coming on.

Suckers can be cut off, with some root if possible, and these too make excellent replacement plants.

When A.V.'s put out their first buds it is wise to remove them, as further blooming will then be more vigorous. For the same reason, remove the top bud from a blooming stem, for it will then produce more flowers. Never, by the way, cut out a leaf from the center of the rosette but take your cuttings from the outside healthy leaves.

Miniature African Violets do very well in terrariums, especially the nonsuckering plants.

When selecting African Violets at a nursery, don't just look for pretty flowers. Consider whether the stems are strong and hold the blossoms up amidst or above the foliage. Look for vigorous leaf growth. Watch for flowers of solid substance and pure color or pattern. One plant among hundreds of the same kind may display a superior vigor which the others do not possess. That is the plant to have. If you find one which performs well for you, hang on to it and multiply it. Discard novelties which behave badly. After a while, and some expense, you will have a nice collection of really satisfactory African Violets. They will afford you a degree of pleasure which hardly any other plant can provide.

· *Seemannia latifolia. Gesneriaceae.* Central America. Terrarium and light gardening plant. Long periods of bloom.

Buy for bloom any time.
HEIGHT: 3 to 6 inches
COLOR OF BLOOM: red-orange
HABIT: upright to spreading and trailing
LIGHT: bright reflected
TEMPERATURE: 65 degrees F. minimum;
 85 degrees maximum
MOISTURE: evenly moist when growing;
 dryish when partially dormant
TRIMMING: remove old blooming stems
PROPAGATION: rhizomes at any time

Seemannia has weak fleshy stems which turn upward at the ends and are topped by a whorl of long, narrow gray-green leaves. The flowers appear singly on three-inch wiry stalks. As with *Hypocyrta,* they have an appearance which is more attractive than our description can suggest. The color is a rich tomato-orange; the length about three-quarters of an inch. Each one consists of a pouched tube (the mouth is narrower than the tube) held in a horizontal position. Due to a very large white stigma sticking out slightly from the roof of the opening, somewhat like a tongue, it has an almost animal look. It takes only a few of these to create a lively and beautiful effect.

Like *Achimenes, Seemannia* is scaly-rhizomatous, but the tubers usually do not go dormant and the plant may bloom for a long time at any time of the year. Excess rhizomes can be worked out of a pot by digging into the soil from the side, and started as new plants by burying them horizontally.

The plant requires quite loose soil and we use Rich Mix without lime, packing it loosely around the rhizome. A condition of high humidity, moderately high temperatures (over sixty-five degrees F. minimum, but not over eighty-five degrees) and soil which is kept moist with as little watering as possible will suit it. We use high phosphate-potash fertilizer. In a terrarium it can be placed twelve inches from the lights but must be within six inches in an open light garden.

Considering these conditions a terrarium is the safest place for *Seemannia*, provided it is not allowed to become too warm. It is not a big plant—it grows only three to six inches high—and increase is by rhizomes which do not develop more than a couple of stems at a time. A four-inch pot is ample even allowing for the desirable spreading of roots. If young plants come up in the pot, you can dig in and take them out so that the parent rhizomes are left uncrowded.

The trouble with a window position is the irregularity of the environment, which seems to disagree with *Seemannia*. Outside a terrarium it will grow best in a cellar light garden where the air is still and conditions are very much the same from day to day. Cool temperatures combined with high humidity will rot the plant.

Seemannia seems to be fairly free of pests; at least we have not had any problems of this sort.

Sinningia 'Cindy' and 'Dollbaby'. *Gesneriaceae*. Everblooming tuberous plants for window, light garden and terrarium.

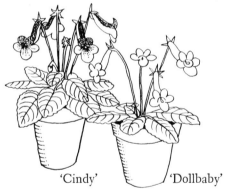

Buy for bloom any time
HEIGHT: 3 inches in bloom
COLOR OF BLOOM: blue and white
HABIT: leafy rosette
LIGHT: partial shade
TEMPERATURE: minimum 65 degrees F.
MOISTURE: evenly moist
PROPAGATION: leaf cuttings. 'Cindy-ella'
   by seed

'Cindy'   'Dollbaby'

What wonders hybridizing can perform! S. 'Dollbaby', which has achieved tremendous popularity, was the product of the mating between S. *pusilla* and S. *eumorpha*, the first a tiny blue-flowered plant, the second a much larger one with six-inch leaves and two-inch-long slipper flowers in white. The result was a medium-size plant with one-and-a-half-inch flowers, lavender blue in color, with the shape of *pusilla*—a flared, five-lobed tube. It also inherited from *pusilla* its everblooming characteristic.

To produce 'Cindy', Thomas Talpey, of Basking Ridge, New Jersey, used the other miniature, *S. concinna* and crossed it with *S. eumorpha*. The same size plant resulted, but the flowers are far prettier than those of 'Dollbaby'. They are white with a broad purple stripe on the top of the tube running into the two upper lobes. The three lower lobes are white, and the throat is lined symmetrically with the same purple dots as *S. concinna*. When in full bloom the plant may have a dozen flowers going at a time, and they seem to arrange themselves as if they wanted their pictures taken. The height is three to four inches.

Originally both 'Dollbaby' and 'Cindy' were sterile, and leaf propagation was very difficult. The story of how 'Dollbaby' was finally made to produce seed varies according to the source, but it *was* accomplished and the fertile form has replaced the sterile one. 'Cindy' was treated with the alkaloid colchicine by Dr. C. William Nixon, of Randolph, Massachusetts, and has also produced viable seed. The fertile plant is called *S.* 'Cindy-ella'. By the time this book is published 'Cindy-ella' will be available to the public.

'Cindy' requires temperatures of sixty-five degrees F. or better to flower regularly, must be kept moist but not soaking wet, and potted in Rich Mix. Start it in a two-and-a-half-inch pot and switch eventually to a four-incher, not because it is so big but because the leaves lie flat and fit comfortably on the surface of a pot that size. It will never bloom on a windowsill or in the light garden so well as in a terrrarium, where it is perfectly happy. This points up its preference for very high humidity and a minimum of actual watering. Remaining just moist is what it wants. Nevertheless it will flower continuously in the open.

On the windowsill, keep it out of direct sunlight. An east window is ideal. Under the lights it should not be more than six inches away, but in a terrarium lighted by fluorescent tubes the distance can be stretched to nearly a foot.

The method of growth of these plants is interesting. Their tubers, which are meant to provide a reservoir of moisture for the plant during the dry spells when it is dormant, produce new growths continuously under the lights. As one stem becomes lax and reaches the limits of its flowerings it can be broken off at the tuber level and a new growth will appear. Thus, in this unique group of plants, the tuber does not inhibit continuous bloom. It is this quality, above all others, which *S. pusilla*

127

and *S. concinna* have generously contributed to this hybrid. Why these little plants should have this characteristic is an interesting question for scientists to answer.

The tiny seed of these plants is sown on a very thin surface of milled sphagnum over Light Mix in a plastic container. Kept close to the lights, it will germinate, can be thinned out into a larger box and then moved to permanent pots.

Because of its perfect size and extreme beauty 'Cindy' is a great acquisition for indoor gardeners.

Sinningia 'Freckles' (fertile form called S. 'Hircon') and 'Bright Eyes'. **Gesneriaceae.** Hybrids. Terrarium plants. 'Freckles' and 'Hircon' will also bloom in the light garden. All three are everblooming.

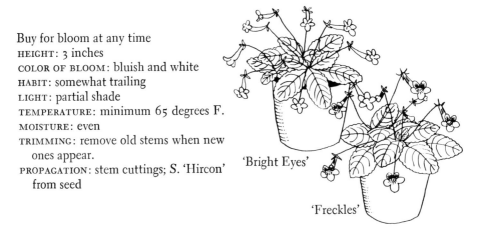

Buy for bloom at any time
HEIGHT: 3 inches
COLOR OF BLOOM: bluish and white
HABIT: somewhat trailing
LIGHT: partial shade
TEMPERATURE: minimum 65 degrees F.
MOISTURE: even
TRIMMING: remove old stems when new
   ones appear.
PROPAGATION: stem cuttings; S. 'Hircon'
   from seed

'Bright Eyes'

'Freckles'

Just as there are an S. 'Dollbaby' and S. 'Cindy' we have here two plants closely related in size and appearance. They are, in fact, about halfway between tiny *pusilla* and *concinna* and the medium-size 'Dollbaby' and 'Cindy'.

'Freckles' has two purple upper lobes, three white lower lobes and a speckled throat. 'Bright Eyes' is light purple above and unmarked white below. The first is rather trailing and the second more compact and upright. As far as culture is concerned they should be treated almost exactly like *S. pusilla* (see p. 130). Both are hybrids created by Dr. Carl D. Clayberg of the Connecticut Agricultural Experiment Station in New Haven. Both plants have become indispensable for flowering terrariums.

S. 'Bright Eyes' is sterile, but S. 'Freckles' has now been made fertile by Dr. Nixon (who did the job on 'Cindy'), and has been given the name S. 'Hircon'. The details we have given about S. 'Cindy' and S. 'Freckles' indicate the rapidity with which developments are taking place in the family and how they come about.

'Freckles' will bloom on the windowsill or in the light garden as long as it has humidity of fifty percent and temperatures of over sixty-five degrees F. 'Bright Eyes' is difficult, except in a terrarium. They both like even moisture and high phosphate-potash fertilizer. Both have larger flowers, grow more lushly and are constantly in bloom in a terrarium. They look best when planted among greenery or with other flowering plants.

Sinningias, Miniature (formerly x *Gloxinera*). Gesneriaceae. Hybrids. Everblooming plants for window, light garden or terrarium.

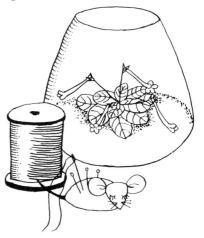

Buy for bloom in the spring
HEIGHT: 3 inches
COLOR OF BLOOM: pink
HABIT: low rosette
LIGHT: bright indirect
TEMPERATURE: minimum 65 degrees F.
MOISTURE: evenly moist until dormant;
    resume watering when tuber sprouts
PROPAGATION: leaf cuttings

Some Miniature Sinningias are a group of artificially created plants resulting principally from the crossing of miniature Sinningias and Rechsteinerias (now also Sinningias).

(Recently Dr. Harold E. Moore of Cornell University proposed the name *Sinningia* for all cultivars previously called x Gloxineras and applied the same epithet to some of the Rechsteinerias. This nomenclature has now been accepted by the American Gloxinia and Gesneriad Society. These Miniature Sinningias [miniature in comparison with *Sinningia speciosa*, the Gloxinia] are, therefore, simply a whole group of very beautiful hybrids with long-tubed trumpet flowers and generally pink coloration.)

In size they fall between the miniature Sinningias and their larger sires. Some are as big as 'Cindy' and 'Dollbaby', some smaller. A great many of these hybrids have not been registered as yet. Among them are some beautifully colored and shaped flowers, but most suffer from the disadvantages of dormancy or sterility, or both. The better ones are taking their place as permanent additions to the indoor gardening repertory, since they are everblooming and attractive. The only real drawback of these plants is that some have a poor leaf habit—the petioles are short and the edges turn under in an unattractive way. Culture is the name as S. 'Cindy'. All are tuberous.

'Connecticut Hybrids', developed by Dr. Carl Clayberg. We have no experience with these plants. They vary in coloration and are fertile.

'Krishna', a hybrid of Mrs. Batcheller's. Long tubed pink flower with nicely flared lobes slightly streaked with darker pink. Everblooming.

'Little Imp', 'Pink Imp', 'Pink Petite'. These are very similar plants, also from Dr. Clayberg. Pink flared tube flowers, compact leaf growth. 'Pink Petite' produces lots of seed spontaneously. Everblooming.

'Pink Flare', Irwin Rosenblum. Almost exactly like a very pink 'Dollbaby'. Everblooming.

Sinningia pusilla. Gesneriaceae. Tropical America. Everblooming miniature for terrarium.

Buy for bloom any time
HEIGHT: maximum 1½ inches
COLOR OF BLOOM: purple
HABIT: flat rosette
LIGHT: partial shade
TEMPERATURE: minimum 65 degrees F.
MOISTURE: just moist
PROPAGATION: self-seeding

This nearly minute plant is an absolute winner with all who come into contact with it. You may wonder why, at first sight. You will see a tiny flat rosette of leaves and a thread of a stem no more than an inch high with a little blue flower, trumpet-shaped, just like a miniaturized *Streptocarpus*. Beneath the leaves in the soil is a little tuber about as big as a pea, at most. By rights this plant should go dormant; it doesn't. On the contrary, it is the most reliable everbloomer we know of and has been a sire for most of our everblooming medium-size Sinningias, which are the wonder of the new house-plant explosion. Moreover, this little fellow forms seedpods readily and sows them all around. Having little root, the plant never becomes a nuisance, and it is always a pleasure to have more of them. Finally, it harbors moss spores for some reason. Everywhere you have a *pusilla* a very fine moss develops all around beneath the leaves.

As long as it is planted in a terrarium, this is the easiest of all the miniatures to bloom, for it needs no attention at all. Just see that the light mix is slightly moist and that the terrarium is closed most of the time so that the plant enjoys high humidity. Don't worry about fertilizer or insects. However, never let the temperature drop below sixty degrees F. or the tuber will rot. It does dislike wet soil. Just moist is right for it.

S. pusilla can be grown in any part of a larger terrarium, or alone or with others in one of its own. A two-tube, twenty-watt fixture eighteen inches above it is sufficient to produce flowering. This means that *pusilla* can be set in the lowest part of a large terrarium in reflected light from any window, remembering that a terrarium should never be in direct sunlight.

The white form of *S. pusilla* is *S.* 'White Sprite', which acts exactly the same as the purple. And Dr. Clayberg has developed a fringed 'White Sprite' which is called 'Snowflake'. With terrariums so popular, *S. pusilla* is a real prize.

The closely related *S. concinna* is a more temperamental plant and even more sensitive to watering and temperature. Give it perfect *S. pusilla* conditions, though, and it too will bloom forever. It has a slightly larger flower, with flatter lobes, and deep purple freckles in the throat. Seed is developed only under controlled humidity conditions.

S. pusilla can go dormant if the soil dries out. We had one planted in a porous rock, which bloomed for a while until we just let the rock and its plants die off. It stayed that way for a year but within a few weeks after it was watered and set in a terrarium, the *pusilla* was blooming again. Sometimes excessive watering or cold may kill off the leaves, but as long as the tuber is healthy all is well. As soon as proper conditions are resumed the plant will go to town.

· **Sinningia speciosa. Gesneriaceae.** Brazil. Gloxinia. Beautiful, rather large-leaved plant for window or light garden. Bloom after period of dormancy.

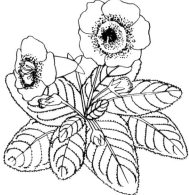

Buy for bloom in bud
HEIGHT: 6 inches in bloom
COLOR OF BLOOM: red, white, blue, speckled, etc.
HABIT: large-leaved rosette—spread to 18 inches
LIGHT: partial sun
TEMPERATURE: minimum 65 degrees F.
MOISTURE: evenly moist when growing; dry during dormancy
PROPAGATION: seeds or leaf cuttings

The Gloxinia has an odd history. The genus name *Gloxinia* belongs properly to a very different plant in the same family but was originally given to the slipper-type Sinningias. And, when, in the 1850s, either in a shipment from Brazil or through hybridization or mutation in a nursery, a kind of *Sinningia* turned up which had a perfectly round shape and equal lobes it was called "Gloxinia," and the name has stuck.

This new plant form became very popular, and the size and coloring of the flowers were greatly improved through hybridization. The old plants still survive in florist-shop windows in spring. The reds are 'Blanche de Meru', 'Emperor Frederick', 'Etoile de Feu' and 'Roi des Rouges'. The purples are 'Emperor William', 'Prince Albert' and 'Royal Velvet'. Usually you see the two handsome "Emperors." These are all very sturdy plants with six to eight inch leaves, with fine showy flowers in clear colors and zonings.

These have become major holiday-gift plants which last a few weeks and then are discarded. For, unfortunately, Gloxinia goes dormant shortly after blooming. Recently, and for the selective buyer, many hybrids have been developed in a bewildering number of colorings and markings. A leader in this field has been Albert Buell of Eastford, Connecticut. The flowers are simply enormous—so large that the stems hardly support them—and the leaves may be a foot in length. Amateurs carry over the bulbs from year to year and constantly rebloom them. There have also been some excellent medium-size doubles. Attempts to dwarf the plant have been only partly successful. Fischer Greenhouses' exquisite 'Tom Thumb' has proved the most reliable.

Although most of these plants have a big spread and the disadvantage of dormancy, they have many admirers. Certainly they are the most spectacular of the gesneriads.

The tubers can be bought at any time of the year. Use Rich Mix with lime and plant in a five- or six-inch azalea pot (shallow). The bottom of the tuber is round and the top has either a scar or an indentation. Set it right side up in the soil and cover with a half inch of the mix. Moisten the soil but do not make it soaking wet. Keep it in a minimum temperature of sixty-five degrees F.

When leaves appear above ground, remove all but one rosette. Place in an east, west or south window where the plant will receive some hours of sunlight. If the leaves reach upward, it is a sign of inadequate light. Directly under the lights is the best position in the light garden and the plant can be slowly moved lower as it grows.

Gloxinias like high humidity and temperatures over sixty degrees F. As soon as growth is well on its way, water the plant thoroughly, then allow it to dry out to the point where the surface of the soil is dry to the touch. Soggy soil can cause the tubers to rot. Fertilize with a high phosphate-potash formula once a week. Be especially careful not to overwater after the buds begin to form.

After blooming for a while, no new buds will form. At this point stop watering gradually until the leaves become yellow. Then break off the flowering stems and leaves and place the pot in a cool dark place. Dormancy lasts six to twelve weeks. During this time the soil should not be allowed to dry out entirely. Water very lightly once every couple of weeks. That means *lightly*, for if you moisten the soil too much the tubers will rot. Don't water the pot through but just around the edges—say, a teacupful.

The tuber will signal the end of dormancy by sprouting. Gently remove it from the soil, rub off the old roots and repot.

With age these tubers can grow six inches in diameter and lose some vigor in the process. The first few bloomings are the best.

Gloxinias are subject to mealybug and a No-Pest Strip is at present the safest cure.

It is easy to fertilize these plants and produce your own seed. Seed germinates rapidly, and plants in a four-inch pot will bloom in about six months.

Streptocarpus. Gesneriaceae. South Africa. Cape Primrose. Window and light-gardening plant with fabulous flowers; blooms continuously.

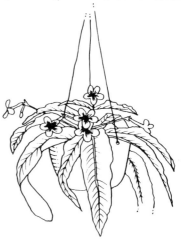

Buy for bloom in fall or early spring
HEIGHT: 6 to 15 inches; spread to 18
   inches
COLOR OF BLOOM: white, pink, red,
   blue, purple
HABIT: long arched leaves
LIGHT: bright indirect
TEMPERATURE: minimum 65 degrees F.;
   not over 85 degrees maximum.
MOISTURE: just moist at all times
PROPAGATION: leaf cuttings, division
   and seed

Amateurs coming across the name *Streptocarpus* for the first time complain that it sounds like a disease. Be that as it may, it is very likely that Streptocarpus disease will create an epidemic of interest in this plant and that it will shortly become the most popular of house plants. There is nothing that matches the elegance of these large flowers, which with good culture are continuous bloomers.

All the major work on these plants has been done in Europe. It started with the *S. rexii* hybrids and continued with the Wiesmoor Hybrids from Germany. Both these strains are available and popular today; they produce beautiful wide-open three-inch flowers, many of them ruffled, on long, arching stems. The colors are white, pink, red, blue and purple, with exquisitely contrasting designs in the throat. We remember one marvelous white with a perfect fleur-de-lis in darkest blue painted on the lower lobe.

For the indoor gardener these plants have presented a challenge because they are rather sensitive to house conditions and require very careful watering. The real breakthrough, in my opinion, has been made by S. 'Constant Nymph', an English hybrid which is somewhat smaller flowered and is characterized by deep-cut lobes and a greater jutting forward of the lower parts of the flower. It is a wonderfully vigorous plant and much easier to grow than the others. Working on 'Constant Nymph', the Dutch have produced a whole series of smaller plants with flowers just as large and in more colors. Now we have 'Netta Nymph', 'Purple Nymph', 'White Nymph', 'Cobalt Nymph'; recently we have seen a 'Red Nymph' listed. Assuredly there will soon be more.

If we describe 'Constant Nymph' the relationship of the other hybrids will be more understandable. It is a stemless plant; that is, the leaves grow directly out of the soil in irregular clumps. Although it starts with two leaves, these soon develop offsets which also multiply, so that a large plant consists of numerous clusters of leaves joined together at the base. The leaves of a full-grown plant are over a foot long, with a rubbly surface and a strong midrib. They are up to three inches broad, the sides almost straight, the tip rounded. They tend to arch.

The peduncles (flowering stalks) grow from the front of the leaf at soil level, rise on strong but thin stems over the top of the foliage, and produce two to six buds which open one by one. The flowers are trumpet-shaped, the lower part jutting forward, and their color a soft, rich blue. The hallmark of the 'Nymph' series is the deeply cleft lobes. Overall flower length is often three inches. Once well established, growth is rapid and large plants may have a dozen stalks blooming at one time, making it one of the most spectacular of exotic plants. Each flower lasts a week or more.

The new Nymphs are smaller plants with six-inch leaves, and therefore are more suitable for confined quarters. The flowers are just as big or bigger than those of 'Constant Nymph'. Whereas the latter soon occupies an eight-inch pot or a big basket, the smaller Nymphs can be accommodated first in a two-and-a-half-incher and later on in a four-incher. Because of its spreading growth these two may eventually occupy large pots but at least the leaves are not so monstrous.

'Netta Nymph' has purple flowers, a pale yellow throat "with a violet-veined blotch." Amateurs report it to be the most floriferous of all the Nymphs. We have had over fourteen flowers blooming for two months with this plant in a two-and-a-half-inch pot. 'Cobalt Nymph', 'White Nymph', etc., are truly descriptive names. All are excellent growers.

We have found little difficulty in growing these plants either in the window or under lights. The juvenile Nymphs will even thrive in a large terrarium for quite a while. But there are a few things to watch in order to have continuous bloom.

The principal need of these Streptocarpus seems to be moderately cool, well-aerated roots and a temperature range from sixty-five degrees F. to eighty degrees. Above eighty and below sixty-five the plant tends to sulk. This means that August and midwinter are dangerous periods. Crown rot can take place if watering is not very carefully controlled at these times. If humidity of fifty percent or better is not maintained, leaves may curl and dry. The plant likes to be misted.

Questions have been raised about proper potting medium and it has been asserted that soilless mixes containing peat are unsatisfactory. We have grown them for a long time in Light Mix without difficulty, and we attribute this to the use of extra lime. Recently we have grown the plants in untreated sphagnum moss and they have reacted even better. When the moss is not packed too tightly around the plants, evaporation is rapid and the roots remain cool even on hot days. This means more watering but is worth it, for the plants seem to thrive. We use high phosphate-potash fertilizer at all times.

In the summer, be sure your plant never dries out. And in winter be sure that the soil or moss is not soaked. That is about all there is to it.

Our "Streps" have had mealybugs at times. The No-Pest Strip or a malathion dip will get rid of them.

The Nymphs are sterile. Propagation from sections of leaf is slow but satisfactory. Cut wedges of leaf and set in moist vermiculite with the mid-vein facing down. They root rather quickly but take a long time to develop new growth.

A better method is division. Decant the plant and soil from the pot and, with a very sharp thin knife, cut away any recognizable clumps of leaves along with some root. These can be potted up, but the side with the wound should be left clear of soil. In other words, leave a depression so that the wound is exposed to the air. Dust the wound with hormone powder or Fermate and fill the depression with perlite. After two weeks, scoop out the perlite and fill with mix. This procedure will prevent fungal diseases.

If you decide to grow some of the more difficult but gorgeous hybrids treat them the same, except that, almost without exception, they must be watered very sparingly. Overwatering produces rot. These plants are slow drinkers and a little moisture goes a long way. If you are careful about watering, you should have magnificent results. We don't think we have ever seen anything finer than a series of baskets of *Streptocarpus*, in many different colors, hanging from the roof of Lyndon Lyon's greenhouse at Dolgeville, New York. The grace of the foliage and the numberless sprays of gay, clean-colored flowers were something to remember.

Haemanthus. Amaryllidaceae. South Africa. Blood Lily. Bulb plant for window or light garden.

Buy for bloom in early spring
HEIGHT: flower stalk 6 to 8 inches high
COLOR OF BLOOM: white, red
HABIT: arching strap leaves
LIGHT: full sun
TEMPERATURE: minimum 60 degrees F.;
    maximum 85 degrees
MOISTURE: Dry August to January;
    moist January to August
PROPAGATION: bulbous offsets

Haemanthus is the most compact of the great South African amaryllids. The flowering is much like that of the showier Alliums—a globe consisting of many individual white or red flowers. In bloom the plant is only six to eight inches high. Later on, the stiff green leaves grow longer, but usually not more than a foot. Flowering is in the spring. But we have seen plants forced to bloom in the fall, and we presume that dormancy was simply extended and some coolness provided during the summer months. For, like all similar plants, *Haemanthus* requires several months of dryness.

Plant the bulbs halfway into Rich Mix with lime, preferably in the form of chips. Set in full sunlight or close to the tubes, and water well, giving a weekly fertilizing of balanced solution. After blooming, the leaves will grow out and the same regimen should continue. But at the end of August dry out the plant completely and set aside until January. Repot every two years, allowing only an extra inch of space around the bulb.

Haemanthus prefers dry air and normal house temperatures. The bulb, if healthy, will produce offsets which can be removed and potted up separately.

Best available species are *H. katharinae* and *coccineus*, red, and *H. albiflos*, white. *H. puniceus*, red, is smaller and requires higher humidity.

Haworthia. Liliaceae. South Africa. Easy succulents for window or light garden.

Buy for bloom in spring
COLOR OF BLOOM: whitish
HEIGHT OF ROSETTE: 2–3 inches;
   flowering stalk 12 inches
HABIT: succulent rosette
LIGHT: partial sun
TEMPERATURE: minimum 65 degrees F.;
PROPAGATION: leaves

The Haworthias mostly form rosettes, from which a flowering stem rises bearing little white flowers usually striped in green. These are not at all showy, but they look right on such a simple plant. None of the Haworthias take up much space—they are satisfied with, at the largest, a two-inch pot—and they form so many offsets that they are easy to propagate, a sort of desert Hen-and-Chickens.

Pot up in Cactus and Succulent Mix and keep moist as long as the

138

temperature is over sixty-five degrees F. and the plants receive plenty of bright light. They *will* burn in hard, direct sunlight in summer. When the temperature drops or when there are cloudy days, let the plants dry out. If they shrivel a bit they will revive as soon as they receive a light watering. Fish emulsion once a month is ample fertilizer.

The most common species are *H. attenuata, fasciata, cymbiformis, margaritifera* and *atrovirens*. Other species will do as well, and the flowers are all much alike.

Hibiscus rosa-sinensis. Malvaceae.   Asia. Hibiscus. Flowering shrub for the sun porch or windowsill.

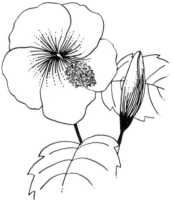

Buy for bloom in spring
HEIGHT: to 6 feet
COLOR OF BLOOM: red, pink, white
HABIT: long-branched, bushy
LIGHT: partial sun
TEMPERATURE: minimum 65 degrees F.;
    maximum 85 degrees
MOISTURE: even
PROPAGATION: stem cuttings

Our experience is with New York City indoor growing, which is as tough as any in the country due to pollution and poor light. South of Washington we have seen *Hibiscus* bloom far back on sun porches or even in well-lighted living rooms. We know Northern city dwellers who have done well with *Hibiscus*. But how well? To bring this plant to bloom occasionally with lots of patience is no great trick. But the flowers last only a couple of days, and unless there is continuous bud production the results are not worth the effort for most people. In the country and farther south it is a satisfactory house plant whose flowers are among the most beautiful of all.

The two principal problems with *Hibiscus* are providing enough light and keeping the plant shapely. In my opinion it should be given the best possible light at all times. For maintenance, house temperatures are well within its normal range. The main thing is to give it a big enough pot so that its roots can spread and the branches grow from which the flowers develop. Thus a ten- to fourteen-inch pot, or even a tub, is not excessive. Use Rich Mix, water and fertilize regularly. Let the plant simply grow out until it flowers, but when the branches get too long, flower or no flower, cut them back and start over again. At temperatures over seventy degrees F. and with good growth you should have bloom.

Hibiscus attracts its quota of insects and a No-Pest Strip hung in the branches is advisable. Propagation is by means of tip growth on branches.

Hippeastrum hortorum. Amaryllidaceae. South America. Amaryllis. One-shot bloomers for the windowsill or sun porch.

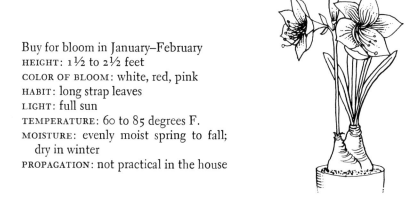

Buy for bloom in January–February
HEIGHT: 1½ to 2½ feet
COLOR OF BLOOM: white, red, pink
HABIT: long strap leaves
LIGHT: full sun
TEMPERATURE: 60 to 85 degrees F.
MOISTURE: evenly moist spring to fall; dry in winter
PROPAGATION: not practical in the house

We were prepared to go into a discussion of the various strains and their blooming seasons, but, from a practical point of view, this would mean very little. Amaryllis will bloom the first time for you, and if they don't, return the bulbs to the grower for credit since all bulbs sold should be foolproof.

Whenever bulbs appear on the market they can be bought with the assurance that bloom will take place four to six weeks after they are planted. Since they are not sold from April to October you can figure that the early winter ones will bloom for Christmas or in January, and the later ones from February to April. You can control the period by simply storing them in a dark cool place until four to six weeks before you want the bloom.

There are very big bulbs nowadays and the best ones will cost five dollars or more. Any well-drained soil will do for them, including our Rich Mix. The pot should be a deep one with a diameter of an inch greater than the maximum diameter of the bulb. Plant the bulb only halfway into the soil and firm the medium well around it. Water regularly, without fertilizing, until bloom is completed.

Normal home temperatures are satisfactory for these plants. Humidity is unimportant except for perfection of bloom. They do last longer and the colors hold up better in a humid atmosphere. Reflected sunlight is quite sufficient for their needs. They are not really dependent upon brightness although colors may be a bit stronger in somewhat brighter light. Direct burning sunlight should be avoided. In early stages of the growth of the flowering stem, bright light should be avoided.

Theoretically you should be able to get a second year's bloom from the bulb by placing it, after flowering, in bright sunlight, watering and fertilizing regularly. In September dry out the bulb completely and keep it that way for at least two months. Then it should be ready for a second go. In actuality only fifty percent of the plants will flower again and the blooms will not be as large.

The Giant Dutch hybrids are mixed colored bulbs, while the Ludwig strain has named varieties. Both are equally good bloomers, but for entering a plant in competition a named variety is an advantage.

If you are thinking of growing these bulbs from seed consider that it takes years to reach maximum size. For the indoor grower it doesn't work.

· *Hoya bella. Asclepiadaceae.*   East Asia. Wax Plant. Shrubby or trailing plant for window or light garden. Chronic bloomer.

Buy for bloom in late spring.
LENGTH: 1 to 2 feet
COLOR OF BLOOM: white
HABIT: trailing, spreading
LIGHT: partial sun
TEMPERATURE: minimum 65 degrees F.
MOISTURE: dry out between waterings
TRIMMING: trim for compact growth
PROPAGATION: stem cuttings

Hoyas are popular principally because of their fleshy, waxy, opposite leaves, which are often prettily variegated—not spotted or banded, but zoned, in pink, white or green. The most familiar is *H. carnosa* and its forms. The original plant has thick green leaves, but those of *H. carnosa exotica* are half yellow and half creamy pink, while *H. carnosa variegata*, the usual one in stores these days, has some leaves combining green and white or, in full sun, brilliant pink. They are slow-growing, large vines which, trained on a trellis or dangling from a basket, will bloom in fall or spring after they have been around a while. *Hoya* is a plant demanding plenty of patience, as it comes into bloom only after it has accustomed itself to an environment.

The flowers, in pendant clusters, are like waxy, shiny stars, some in warm brown and red shades and others, like *H. bella*, glistening white with pink centers. They are exquisitely perfumed and long-lasting. All the Hoyas can be pruned and trained easily, but they have a peculiarity which you must consider. When the flower cluster dies, a short peduncle (flowering stem) remains, which should not be disturbed, for it is from this that further flowering takes place. So, in trimming the plant, you must make up your mind whether to save these stem branches or sacrifice them for the sake of good plant shape in the hope that new branches will grow out and produce new peduncles.

Certainly the easiest-blooming of a number of Hoyas in cultivation is *H. bella*. Indeed, we grow it for bloom alone as its foliage is nothing special. The stems are wiry and stiff and the opposite leaves are less than an inch long and pointed. They too are stiff, but not waxy or thick. It behaves more like a shrub, putting out branches in every direction and usually grows no more than ten inches high and fifteen inches across in a well-cultured plant. It is not easy to train, but we have seen plants which were a perfect round with branches loaded with clusters of bright flowers. The secret is even lighting all around, which is much more available in a greenhouse than in a window. Under lights it would take up too much room in a central position. Usually, therefore, you will see it growing out on one side toward the light.

Although accustomed in nature to brilliant light, Hoyas receive enough to bloom in an east window or somewhat out of direct light in a south or west exposure. They should be potbound in Light Mix with lime and fertilized with a high phosphate-potash formula. Allow them to dry out completely between waterings. Temperatures should be sixty degrees F. or higher, but the humidity requirement is low. During cloudy or cool periods, be very sparing with the water.

The vine Hoyas must be staked or trellised if allowed to grow large. But we have seen some that were virtually bonsaied, growing stems no more than six inches long, yet bearing blooms. To accomplish this the plant must be kept rather dry during growth periods and in good light so that the stems do not grow too rapidly or far.

H. bella, if it is happy, will bloom cyclically throughout the year. However, most of the bloom is on new growth and eventually you must trim back. If the peduncles on the plant are in good shape, flowers will appear again on the more compact plant and eventually you will be able to remove all new growth as it appears.

Mites have a field day with these plants, as do mealybugs.

* *Impatiens balsamina. Balsaminaceae.* Tropical Asia. Garden Balsam. An annual plant which will bloom for months in summer or winter with little attention. Rather short-lived.

Buy for bloom in spring
HEIGHT: 12 inches
COLOR OF BLOOM: pink, white, red
HABIT: erect, bushy
LIGHT: full sun
TEMPERATURE: minimum 60 degrees F.
MOISTURE: even
PROPAGATION: seed or stem cuttings at
   any time

The taller varieties of Garden Balsam can be grown indoors but look out of place. They have thick fleshy stems, rather bare near the ground and broadening out into crowded foliage farther up. In the garden they seem nicely proportioned because we are looking down on them. But at home, where the scale is altogether different, they look incongruous and they become positively ugly if, due to the lower light intensity, they become elongated. Dwarf varieties, however, are suitable and more successful.

Continual hybridization has produced numerous strains which, as always, differ somewhat in height, coloring and adaptability. The double-flowered types are showier and last longer on the plant. If you choose variety according to your own preferences you will still have pretty good results. Heights range from about ten to fifteen inches in the dwarf kinds.

Buy seed in the spring and plant indoors or out; pot the plants up and bring them indoors to grow and bloom at the window or under lights. For winter flowering, plant in late August. In the city, the plants need maximum light at the window as well as under lights if growth is to be compact. In a bright country window they thrive on indirect light. The pots should be deep four- or five-inchers, with Light Mix. Water moderately, allowing the plants to dry out between, and give them a daily mild dose of balanced fertilizer. If lower leaves start to rot, spray the plants with Benlate or Benomyl. By pinching off the side branches you can keep the plant neat, short and capable of producing more bloom. They don't mind heat, and also will tolerate fifty-five degrees F. at night on occasion without dropping their flowers. Figure on four to six months of active service from this plant.

This *Impatiens* sets seed rather easily. The capsules explode amusingly when pressed between the fingers and, as children, we used to enjoy the feel of them curling up in our hands and seeing the seeds tossed some distance by the spring action. But once you have a variety you prefer, it is much easier to take branch cuttings so the plants will come true. In winter *Impatiens* may need supplementary light during cloudy periods at the window.

These are easy plants but do require a fair amount of light. Under fluorescent lamps they need a pretty central position with the tops about three inches from the tubes.

Impatiens sultanii. Balsaminaceae.   East Africa. Impatiens. Easy perennial for window or light garden. Everblooming.

Buy plants for bloom in spring
HEIGHT: 6–24 inches, depending on
    variety
COLOR OF BLOOM: pink, white, red
HABIT: bushy
LIGHT: partial sun
TEMPERATURE: minimum 60 degrees F.
MOISTURE: even
TRIMMING: prune for bushiness
PROPAGATION: seed in spring or fall;
    stem cuttings at any time

Impatiens sultanii and *Impatiens holstii* have been bred for so long that the parentage of the modern plants no longer counts. But in our seed catalogues the Sultanas are the smaller plants—up to fifteen inches—and the taller ones are usually called Holstii hybrids. For the house those listed as "extra dwarf" varieties (six to ten inches high) and the so-called Hybrida Nana (six inches high) are the best.

Plants are easy to come by in the spring, but if you want the best winter bloom it is advisable to start with seed. Plant in August or early September on top of the soil in light. Germination is fifteen days.

Pot up in Rich Mix with lime, give full sun or your best spot under the lights, keep moist and in 50 percent humidity, feed regularly, and you will have constant bloom. It is best to treat *Impatiens* as an annual and take cuttings to get fresh young plants. Prune to encourage bushiness.

Impatiens comes in a wide range of colors, which are a bit flat and watery. But occasionally a plant will have deeper, richer color. Tangerine grows fifteen inches tall and is the handsomest of these plants, both for leaves and shape of flower. There are also one-foot doubles, if you like them.

The plants will do best in an air-conditioned apartment or anywhere the temperatures can be kept lower than the eighties, but you should give them a minimum of sixty degrees F. They are subject to red spider mites, which often come with the seed itself.

145

* *Ixora. Rubiaceae.* India, China and the East Indies. Everblooming shrub for window or light garden.

Buy for bloom in spring
HEIGHT: 12–30 inches
COLOR OF BLOOM: orange, yellow, red
HABIT: bushy
LIGHT: partial sun
TEMPERATURE: minimum 65 degrees F.
TRIMMING: Prune for bushiness
PROPAGATION: stem cuttings at any time

Everywhere in Florida you can see *Ixora* used as a hedge. A medium-sized shrub, it branches a great deal and produces rounded heads of four-petaled flowers in shades of orange, pink, red and yellow. The preferred hedge types grow four feet high, but there are smaller varieties which are better for the house, such as 'Superking', a low form called *I.* 'Rosea', and *I.* 'Westii' (Alberts & Merkel).

Contrary to most of our tropical house plants, *Ixora* requires acid conditions similar to *Rhododendron* or *Gardenia*. Rich Mix without lime is therefore called for and fertilizer should be high in nitrates. If the leaves do not remain a deep green you will have to add some chelated iron in the form of Sequestrene and a teaspoon of ammonium sulphate per gallon of water for three or four waterings. A second requirement is plenty of warmth. Don't expose it to less than sixty-five degrees F. Use room-temperature water at all times and fertilize more heavily than your other plants—the manufacturer's label recommendation can be followed here. As it need not grow very high, but does bush out a lot, a fairly large pot must be used as it matures—six- and even ten-inchers are in order.

In regard to light the new Ixoras are not as demanding as older varieties; they may be placed out of direct sunlight in the window and about twelve inches below the lights. But the plants will not bloom in the window unless there are plenty of sunny days; otherwise they need supplementary artificial light. If you have a young plant, nip it back aplenty to make it bush and produce more flower heads. These latter

146

must be removed as they fade. In this respect it is the same as *Lantana*, whose blooming cycles are followed by the formation of a new set of buds; this must be encouraged by removal and trimming.

Your purchased plant, like so many others, will lose its flowers shortly after you bring it home. This is caused by the shock of changed environment. So don't move it during flowering periods. Get it set in one place and leave it there unless you feel that it lacks the right light or temperature. Then you will have to move it and be patient until it recovers. Once it feels at home, you are in for years of beautiful bloom.

Allow to dry out partially between waterings but spray frequently to encourage growth and bloom. If your plant stops blooming in the window, which usually happens in winter, reduce watering drastically.

Propagation is not difficult from young stem cuttings in moist vermiculite any time during warm weather.

· *Jacobinia carnea. Acanthaceae.*   Brazil. Window or light garden. Intermittent bloom all year.

Buy for bloom in spring or fall
HEIGHT: 4 to 12 inches in the house
COLOR OF BLOOM: pink
LIGHT: partial sun
TEMPERATURE: minimum 65 degrees F.
MOISTURE: just moist; do not wet
TRIMMING: prune to keep small
PROPAGATION: stem cuttings at any time

When we first saw *Jacobinia carnea* in a botanical garden it was big, scraggly and unsightly, in spite of its spectacular spikes of pink flowers. It didn't occur to us that it would one day become one of our favorite house plants. Then we gambled on a young plant, brought it home and placed it in a south window. It was so ornery, threatening to give up the ghost at any moment, that we nicknamed it "Trouble." Returning from a vacation, we found that it had indeed expired but were told by our plant-sitter that it had bloomed with its last breath—confirming its

contrariness. When we took up light gardening we gave *Jacobinia* another try. We now have learned to know it better and to appreciate its
virtues if handled right.

Jacobinia has irregularly quilted thin green leaves up to six inches
long. If the single stalk of a young plant is nipped at the top, thick hairy
stems grow out like a candelabrum and the plant can be kept quite
compact. The flowering heads look at first like narrow green pine cones,
so thickly packed are the green bracts. Then the flowers peek out,
elongate and finally open; they are about two inches in length with a
long upper lobe and an almost equally long lower one curved downward
and divided into three very short lobes. The many-flowered cluster is
often four or five inches long. Flowering lasts for a couple of weeks.

Our real breakthrough with this plant occurred when we found out
how easy it was to propagate and how quickly the flowers developed on
the new growth. Cut off two or three nodes at the end of a branch and
plant directly into Rich Mix at any time of year. Moisten the soil well
and cover plant and pot with a plastic bag for a couple of days in semishade. Some leaves may drop off in the first few days but new ones should
start to grow out almost immediately. As soon as removal of the bag no
longer causes leaves to become limp, the plant can be set within a few
inches of the lights or in a partially sunny position on a windowsill. The
soil should be kept moist at all times during the first period.

What happens now is quite unusual. On a stem which may still
carry only a couple of leaves, a bud cluster appears, soon elongates and,
in a few weeks, flowers. Often the spike is longer than the stem. When
flowering is over, remove the spike immediately. It is brittle and breaks off
neatly at the node. Immediately the stem will start to branch and new
buds will begin to form at the tips. The question now is how big you
want the plant to grow. That is up to you. We don't let ours get over
twelve inches, preferring to start new plants when the base of an old
one, after a number of flowerings, becomes woody.

Proceeding in this way you can have flowers all year round under
lights. In the window the bloom is more seasonal—mostly from May to
August. In winter, bloom is inhibited by the short days. A plant kept in
the window in summer and put under the lights in winter will continue
to bloom. Essentially this is true of other windowsill plants as well.

There are two other requirements for *Jacobinia*. It must have warm temperatures—sixty-five degrees F. and higher. Watering has to be done very carefully. This is one of those plants whose leaves turn brown and whose flowers blast if it is overwatered. It should be kept just moist—if anything, on the dry side—between waterings. If you happen to give too little water and the spike begins to droop even while in bud, a small amount of liquid will revive it and it will be none the worse.

Jacobinia does not require high humidity but benefits from it. Use 20-20-20 fertilizer. Under the lights, it will bloom as far away as 15 inches. On the windowsill it prefers partial sun, except in the city, where it needs pretty much the maximum you can give it. Our plants have never had pests.

You can grow *J. carnea* this way very comfortably in four-inch pots. If you use larger ones, expect it to grow two or three feet high, whereupon its branches will become weak and unsightly. A small plant is much more decorative. If it is carefully grown for display, you can force four or five tremendous clusters on stems no more than three or four inches high.

Beat that!

· *Jasminum sambac* '**Maid of Orleans**'. *Oleaceae.*   India. Fragrant vine blooming off and on, and not very easy to grow.

Buy for bloom in spring
HEIGHT: 12 inches
COLOR OF BLOOM: white
HABIT: bushy vine
LIGHT: partial shade
TEMPERATURE: minimum 65 degrees F.
MOISTURE: constantly moist
TRIMMING: keep small by pruning
PROPAGATION: stem cuttings at any time

Some like it cold, some like it hot. The last applies to *Jasmine 'Sambac'*. Time and again people have asked, "Why doesn't my Jasmine bloom?" Answer: "Not warm enough."

The almost bush growth and fragrant tube-and-pinwheel flowers in purest white are the reason for the popularity of this vine. But do not count on flowers unless the temperature is over seventy degrees F. and the humidity high. Obviously, in most houses, summer flowering is all that can be expected. Keep it pruned to a maximum of 12 inches at all times.

Use Rich Mix and keep moist. Fertilize with fish emulsion. If you can give it terrarium conditions, so much the better. It will bloom in an environment where other plants would suffocate. Keeping this in mind, you may be successful.

There are other jasmines also worth trying. Some of these are not true jasmines but are usually listed along with them as being trumpet-shaped, fragrant and vines or small shrubs—for instance, *Cestrum diurnum* and *nocturnum* from the West Indies and *Gelsemium sempervirens*, the Carolina Jessamine. These require moderate light and just moist soil. Temperatures of over sixty-five degrees F. are also a requirement. They are unreliable bloomers in the house.

Jatropha. Euphorbiaceae. American tropics. Windowsill plant and possibly light garden.

Buy for bloom in early spring
HEIGHT: up to 24 inches
COLOR OF BLOOM: red
HABIT: erect, spreading
LIGHT: full sun
TEMPERATURE: minimum 65 degrees F.
MOISTURE: just moist, not wet
TRIMMING: cut off branching growth to
    keep in check
PROPAGATION: division of offshoots;
    stem cuttings

The Jatrophas are among the "new" plants and bid fair to become much more popular as new species are introduced and new cultivars developed. *J. podagrica* has a grotesque, swollen, tapering trunk, and can grow to about two feet. It has attractive segmented leaves and brilliant clusters of small red flowers blooming throughout the year as long as it is given plenty of sun and humidity. Being a slow grower, it is not much favored by the nurseries, so grab it when the opportunity presents itself.

J. multifida has very showy, finely cut leaves. The flower clusters are coral red.

J. pandurifolia 'Dwarf' is a shrubby plant with simple leaves. The individual flowers are larger than those of the two other species and fewer in number.

Grow Jatrophas in Light Mix in your brightest exposure—direct sun if possible. Humidity should be forty percent or more. Though they flourish best in very bright light, they are quite tolerant of lower intensities and are worth trying in reflected light and under the fluorescent lamps. Keep moist during sunny warm periods and cut down the moisture when the temperature drops or cloudy days intervene. Fertilize with a balanced formula every two weeks in the warm months and once a month in winter. Jatrophas tolerate drought but require moisture to retain leaves and to flower. House temperatures as low as sixty degrees F. are fine.

Grow new plants from the large seeds, which germinate in ten days, or from branch cuttings.

The interesting shape of the Jatrophas and the extraordinary brilliance of the small flowers make them very desirable in the house.

• *Lagerstroemia indica. Lythraceae.*   China. "Crape Myrtlette." Shrubby plant for window or light garden.

Buy for bloom at any time
HEIGHT: to 15 inches
COLOR OF BLOOM: red, pink, mauve,
    white
HABIT: shrubby
LIGHT: sun
TEMPERATURE: minimum 65 degrees F.
MOISTURE: moist but not wet
TRIMMING: constant pruning of
    branches to make plant bush
PROPAGATION: stem cuttings and seed

Dwarf varieties of Crape Myrtle have been known for a long time. But until Park Seed Company introduced Crape Myrtlettes, it was not a really suitable house plant. The new strain is very dwarf and may be as satisfactory a blooming shrub as *Cuphea hyssopifolia,* which belongs to the same family.

The Crape Myrtlettes must be started from seed at a temperature of minimum sixty-five degrees F. Germination may take a month, but buds will appear when the plant is only two inches high, in about ten weeks. These should be removed to encourage growth and branching.

The leaves are an inch long, paired along the weak branches, which nod and keep the plant reasonably low for a long time. It is safe to let your Crape Myrtle bloom when it has a branch four or five inches long. The effect is astonishing, for the compound flower is two inches across, consisting of a circle of eight to ten ruffled petals, attached to a capsule as big as a pea by stiff, wiry little stalks. The colors are snow-white, lavender, pink and red. The shades you like can be propagated from stem cuttings at any time.

Crape Myrtle will thrive in a south or west window in full sun, or in the center of the light garden up to four inches below the tubes. Keep moist but not soggy for the plant is sensitive to excess moisture. If it starts to droop when the soil is wet, let the pot dry out well. Pot in Rich Mix with lime and fertilize with a high phosphate-potash formula. Move from smaller to larger pots as the plant grows, but trim back the branch tips to make it more bushy. It prefers humidity of over fifty percent. Remove the flower capsules as soon as bloom is finished. A fantastically floriferous plant—and easy!

• *Lantana nana compacta. Verbenaceae.* Tropical America. Everbloomer on windowsill and in the light garden.

Buy for bloom at any time
HEIGHT: 4 to 12 inches
COLOR OF BLOOM: zoned red, white, orange-pink
HABIT: shrubby
LIGHT: full sun
TEMPERATURE: minimum 65 degrees F.
MOISTURE: keep very wet
TRIMMING: prune back after blooming
PROPAGATION: stem cuttings

The familiar *Lantana camara* is a coarse, hairy plant which grows very large if given the chance and produces an endless series of multiflowered blooms consisting of concentric rows in different hues. There are myriad color variations and combinations. It makes a good garden plant and a splendid basket plant for hanging on a porch in summer where the white flies it attracts by the million will bother nobody. It is something of a joke that the most popular of the basket plants are Fuchsias and Lantanas, both of which are the favorites of these insects. Rightly, it is not considered a good indoor plant because of its rank growth and the flies. The more delicate *Lantana montevidensis*, bearing exclusively lilac flowers, is not quite that easy a plant and doesn't compare with *Lantana nana compacta*.

Dwarf Lantanas come in the same color variations as their large relatives but are much less coarse, more adaptable in every way, and just as floriferous and pretty. For us they have not attracted white flies as persistently as the others.

By all means get plants from a nursery, being sure to specify the compact variety. Seed takes a long time to germinate—often fifty days or more—and this is a delay to which indoor growers don't take kindly. Small plants in bloom, chosen for their colors, will meet your needs. And cuttings taken from these root in moist vermiculite with exemplary speed and ease. Also, the time to blooming is cut down drastically.

Culture is of the simplest. On the windowsill, put the plant in the brightest possible position. Under lights a distance of 12 inches is tolerated. Water plentifully and regularly. The plants have a reputation for drought resistance, but they will stop blooming and lose their leaves if dried out. Fertilize with a balanced formula. Humidity is unimportant and temperatures can be anything over fifty degrees F. Bloom takes place cyclically throughout the year. This has to do with the trimming process, which is all-important.

The habit of *Lantana*—even the compact variety—is to grow longer and longer branches and to bloom periodically from the new leaf rosettes at the tips. In the house, after each blooming, trim the plant back neatly, whereupon it will branch more and bear a new set of blooms. Repeat the process each time. Thus you will have bloom for a few weeks, a cutting back, new growth, and bloom again. The intervals are about six weeks. If side branches are removed and the top trained to shape, you can easily make a neat little tree. The plant has not been used for bonsai but is very adaptable to that purpose and more people should be doing it. When in bloom, a well-shaped *Lantana* of this type is a real show plant and a delight to behold.

• ***Lobelia erinus. Lobeliaceae.*** South Africa. Lobelia. Annual basket or pot plant for window or light garden.

Buy for bloom in the spring
HEIGHT: 1 to 2 inches
COLOR OF BLOOM: blue, white, red
HABIT: spreading, trailing
LIGHT: partial sun
TEMPERATURE: 60 to 80 degrees F.
MOISTURE: just moist
TRIMMING: cut off trailing ends
PROPAGATION: from seed at any time

The marvelously blue little garden edging plant makes an excellent pot plant at any time of year. Grow from seed planted below soil level and figure on bloom in eight weeks. You can have Lobelias flowering right through the winter, taking up little space and supplying a great mass of rich color. Calculate three plants to a four-inch pot.

The new varieties such as 'Blue Stone' (true blue), the white 'White Lady' and the red 'Rosamund', to mention only a few of the strains, form little mounds, their sides trailing over the edges of the pot. In the house the pots may have to be supported.

Use Rich Mix with double the normal quantity of lime, water well at all times and fertilize with high phosphate-potash solution. Place in bright indirect light, or four inches below the tubes. Lobelia likes cool roots so a basket or a clay pot may suit them better than a plastic pot. When the plants are full grown in the pot there should be no space between their foliage. It is better to potbind them. Don't expect more than four or five months of bloom.

154

·*Malpighia coccigera. Malpighiaceae.* West Indies. Barbados Holly. Window and light garden. Perennial. Chronic bloomer.

Buy for bloom in the spring
HEIGHT: 4 to 12 inches
COLOR OF BLOOM: pink
HABIT: woody shrub
LIGHT: partial sun
TEMPERATURE: minimum 60 degrees F.
MOISTURE: keep moist, not wet
TRIMMING: prune branches to shape
PROPAGATION: cuttings from young
  wood

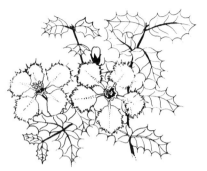

Few people can resist this plant, which, when well grown, is a neat small shrub (a foot high at most), very branched, with a myriad of sharply pointed, shiny little leaves exactly like those of holly, and absolutely blanketed by exquisite one-inch pink flowers. These blossoms, lying flat on the branches, have five irregularly sized, prettily fringed, roundish petals on little stalks. It is a moot point whether some of the famous equitant *Oncidium* orchids mimic *Malpighia* or the other way round. Under ultraviolet photography both appear to offer the same pattern to a visiting bee. As for the holly leaves—could that be mimicry too?

We killed many Malpighias before we found a plant which behaved for us and which we continue to propagate. It remains an open question whether this was a matter of clone (a particular plant) or whether we have unconsciously solved the problem of growing it. It is well known that plants rooted and brought up from Florida are very susceptible to fungus, but it may be that our plant was well acclimated at the time we acquired it. A nurseryman once expressed his desire to get his hands on any northern-grown plants in quantity. And this seems to confirm that the problem has something to do with change of environment. Anyway our plants now bloom profusely and we have no further troubles, although a city apartment is certainly a tough environment for any plant.

This is not very encouraging for the average grower. But we suggest looking around in nurseries for plants which have been propagated locally rather than brought up from the South, as these are likely to be more adaptable. Nurseries have the habit of planting them in sandy soil. Get rid of this and plant in Light Mix with a very liberal addition of lime. Outdoors, the plants grow in Florida in sand plus shell. For the house, our mix is much more satisfactory, as sand dries out immediately. One other point: your plant may, for quite a while, have oval rather than holly leaves. Don't worry. These are the immature ones and the others will appear in due time.

Deciding what moisture Malpighia tolerates was not easy. In the long run we found that we could water it quite regularly and keep it really moist but not swimming, as long as there was good growth and plenty of sunlight or artificial light. The temperature should be over sixty degrees F. It will tolerate less, but when this happens cut down sharply on the watering, otherwise the plant will rot. We keep the Malpighias in maximum four-inch pots so that they do not grow over ten inches high. Any bigger, and they must have quite a large one—say, an eight-incher at least. High phosphate and potash fertilizer applied regularly encourages bloom, especially in early spring. It flowers off and on throughout the rest of the year, but less profusely.

In the window give them an eastern exposure, and under lights place them about a foot away. In a south or west window keep them out of the full sunlight most of the time.

Our plants have had infestations of mealybugs, cured by dunking in malathion. Other pests don't seem to bother them.

Malpighia is a woody plant and as it grows older develops a solid trunk, which makes it superb material, with its small leaves, for bonsaiing. Nevertheless, cuttings of young, firm wood root rather easily in moist vermiculite. Thin or young branches seem to be more susceptible to rot, and don't take as well. The plant does have a pretty red fruit, but our flowers have never been fertilized, and this would appear to be rather difficult in the house.

Malpighia seems to thrive in moderate humidity but dislikes a combination of high humidity and still air. It is a frequent sufferer in August. Moving air seems to agree with it.

Even without flowers *Malpighia* is a beautiful plant—a joy to train and to pot in an attractive manner.

Manettia bicolor. Rubiaceae. Firecracker Vine. Tropical America. Small vine for window or light garden.

Buy for bloom in the spring
HEIGHT: 6 to 12 inches if trimmed
COLOR OF BLOOM: scarlet and yellow
HABIT: slender vine
LIGHT: reflected light
TEMPERATURE: minimum 70 degrees F.
MOISTURE: moderately wet
TRIMMING: cut back vine to bush
PROPAGATION: stem cuttings

If drastically pruned this little vine will become quite bushy and grow no more than six to eight inches high, bearing numerous one-inch scarlet tube flowers tipped with yellow. Allowed to run, it will twine up a stake or a string for a few feet.

Manettia requires temperatures of seventy degrees or higher, humidity fifty percent or higher, plenty of moisture, and bright reflected light. If grown in the light garden, keep the vine close to the tubes to start with. These are conditions which we used to consider pure greenhouse, but are now possible in many homes with humidifiers and well-controlled, comfortable temperatures in winter.

The plant, with its delicate leaves, is rather subject to green aphids and white fly, so keep a No-Pest Strip nearby.

Marigold. *Compositae.* South America. *Tagetes* species and hybrids. An easy and long-lasting house plant for windowsill or light garden.

Buy seeds for bloom all year
HEIGHT: dwarfs 6 to 12 inches
COLOR OF BLOOM: yellow, orange
HABIT: upright
LIGHT: full sun
TEMPERATURE: minimum 60 degrees F.
MOISTURE: just moist
TRIMMING: remove dead flowers
PROPAGATION: seed at any time

There is no point in using the Latin name in this case, as the Marigold has become quite divorced from its habitat and now forms a part of the great modern outdoor garden syndrome of Marigolds, Zinnias and Petunias—the plants one grows if too lazy to tackle anything else.

It is amazing how well it does in the house, especially under lights, considering that it is the plant par excellence for the hot, dry July–August season out of doors. Once it becomes popular indoors, seedsmen will be selling seeds in the fall instead of exclusively in the spring. For this is a plant which can grow and bloom for you any time of the year.

Popularity in the garden is as much due to its ease of culture, which is equivalent to that of a field weed, as to the handsome yellow to orange flowers. The seed is almost always reliable and can be planted directly into Light Mix in a three- or four-inch pot. Naturally we do not recommend choosing the seed of the giant-flowered, two-foot plants. Happily the trend is toward miniatures, even in the garden, and many varieties are available. The small plants will work proportionally much bigger in the house.

Using Park Seed Company catalogue as a guide, we note the Petite Marigold series, the Dwarf French and the Cupid Marigolds, all of which offer a large number of shades and forms. Pick the kinds which normally grow under twelve inches tall.

As soon as Marigolds start to bud they should not be allowed to bloom immediately but should be pinched back to achieve maximum bushiness. Then let them go. If you follow the cultural directions they will bloom profusely, and each flower will last as long as a month in the house. After six months or so the branches will get woody and less productive, but by that time you can have new ones. Figure six weeks from seed to bloom and you will not go far wrong. Thus, if you plan carefully, you can have Marigolds right through the year.

Naturally you have to give them a sunny window—a south or west exposure without protection. Even then, a period of cloudy days will cause the plants to make vegetative growth rather than bloom. The risk is greater in winter, and in the city more than in the country. Under lights the long day length seems to compensate adequately for sun, and they do very well as much as twelve inches from the lights.

Humidity and normal house temperatures are no problem. Allow to just dry out between waterings, but don't neglect them as they have shallow roots and will fade quickly if underwatered. Give them regular feedings of balanced fertilizer.

We have found them susceptible to mites in a big way and equally so to a No-Pest Strip if it is too close to the plant. Leaves will shrivel if the strip is hung within six inches of it. That is also one of the problems of city growing, for it also seems sensitive to heavy pollution. However these problems can be solved and your Marigolds will usually flourish. The best way to get rid of the mites under the circumstances is to dip the plant in a solution of Kelthane a few times at weekly intervals.

Nerine. Amaryllidaceae.   South Africa. Guernsey Lily. Pretty bulbs for window or light garden.

Buy in the fall for winter bloom
HEIGHT: to 18 inches
COLOR OF BLOOM: pink, crimson
HABIT: erect bulb plant
LIGHT: full sun
TEMPERATURE: minimum 65 degrees F.
MOISTURE: dry May to September;
  moist September to May.
PROPAGATION: offsets

Nerines have the advantage of being winter-flowering and can be potted up in the fall with half the bulb covered. Rich Mix with lime will do. Do not water until growth starts, then keep the plant moist and fertilize once a week with fish emulsion until bloom, which, depending on the species, will be anytime from November to January. High humidity and bright light are required and the temperature should not be below sixty-five degrees F., so it will do very well along with tropical flowering plants in the light garden. *Nerine* has leaves which don't take much room.

The scape grows up to one and a half feet and bears an umbel of crisp flowers in pink to crimson. Species are N. *bowdenii*, N. *curvifolia*, N. *fothergillii* and N. *sarniensis*. The last two are the taller ones and not recommended for the light garden.

From May until September the bulbs should dry in or out of their pots and the mix can be changed in August.

• **Nerium oleander. Apocynaceae.** Southern Europe. Oleander. Large shrub for window. Has been grown and bloomed under lights.

Buy for bloom in spring
HEIGHT: to 5 feet
HABIT: long-caned shrub
LIGHT: full sun
TEMPERATURE: minimum 60 degrees F.
MOISTURE: just moist
TRIMMING: cut canes back for bushiness
PROPAGATION: stem cuttings

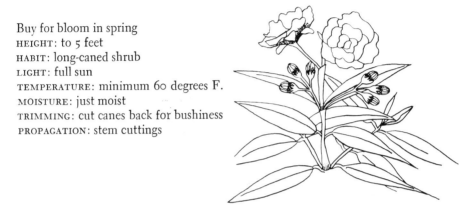

Oleander, being extremely poisonous in all its parts, is not a plant for a house with undiscriminating cats or children who have to experiment with the alimentary properties of everything around them. We used to think that warnings against the eating of such plants were superfluous, on the grounds that it should be easy to prevent their consumption. However, it appears that urban cats and children equally lack a sense of discrimination, and that more often than one would believe possible, the latter, especially, turn up at doctors' offices and hospitals in the company of frantic parents after a rather unusual meal. So take warning.

There are any number of different color variations available ranging from single white blooms to double reds. The problem is not to find the right color, but the best plant for the house. Unfortunately this requires considerable experimentation and we cannot give you a lead on this point. If you buy a juvenile plant, give it your sunniest position. Eventually it would be wise to repot in Rich Mix. Keep it moist except during cool periods, when it can be allowed to dry out between waterings. Going easy on fertilizer will prevent it from growing out of hand. This is a big shrub and needs lots of root space, so figure on a 12-inch pot as a minimum if you desire to flower it.

You do have to let it grow out during the summer, but in the fall it is possible to trim it back severely so that the next year it will not already be a monster. This is especially needed under lights. With care you will have blooms rather regularly. This is a plant which will take quite a beating, but reliable blooming in the house depends on circumstances. Once flowering has started it is pretty continuous.

• *Ochna multiflora. Ochnaceae.* Tropical Africa. Small tree for the window.

Buy for bloom in spring
HEIGHT: to 3 feet in the house
COLOR OF BLOOM: yellow with red calyx
HABIT: branched woody shrub
LIGHT: full sun
TEMPERATURE: minimum 60 degrees F.
MOISTURE: keep moderately wet
TRIMMIMG: trim to keep small
PROPAGATION: stem cuttings

Ochna is quite different from most of our indoor shrubs and small trees. It grows slowly from seed and usually does not reach blooming size for a year. We have seen it as a thin-stemmed tree, two and a half feet high, with a few woody branches, not many of its narrow leaves and a generally rather naked appearance. But, when pruned back when small it can also be more compact and leafy—no more than a foot high. In early spring it starts producing pendant bright yellow flowers with numerous yellow stamens, very much like large *Hypericum* blossoms. These last but a few days. What is much more fascinating now takes place. A bright red fleshy receptacle appears, almost like raw meat in appearance, and on this develop the at first green, then deep black, shiny seeds, three to five in number. The seeds stay on for weeks and the receptacle even longer. This goes on for several months and is most unusual in appearance. (Logee's Greenhouses has plants.)

Culture is very simple, for all it needs is house temperatures, moderate watering, occasional high-nitrate fertilizer and full sun—the more the better. Use Rich Mix without lime. You can grow more plants from your own seed or from cuttings of young wood.

ORCHIDS

Here are a few statistics on this most varied of flowering plants. The number of species is estimated as from twenty to fifty thousand, the second largest among the families. Orchids grow all over the world between the Arctic and the Antarctic, from sea level up to ten thousand feet, on trees and in the ground. There are even a couple, in Australia, which grow underground. They are entirely dependent on insects for pollination and have developed the most intricate methods for attracting them and forcing them to carry their pollinia. Many are deliciously perfumed, others odorless, and not a few absolutely foul-smelling. The seedpods may contain several million seeds. Since the seeds possess no endosperm (storage food), they depend in nature on a fungus parasite and in cultivation on being treated very much like a bacterial culture.

If you know only the corsage orchids, you should visit an orchid nursery where numerous species and hybrids are displayed. There is just nothing like it. Some of the flowers last only a day; others are among the most long-lasting. Single flowers have been known to stay fresh for four months or more.

A large number of orchids have been grown successfully on the windowsill or in the light garden by amateurs. However, most growing has been in the greenhouse, and indoor growing of flowering plants, especially in the light garden, is comparatively new. Thus we are not as yet very well informed about which of the thousands of species and the equal number of cultivars are really dependable performers for the average house-plant grower.

The study of orchids can easily occupy one for a lifetime. Just getting to know all the kinds is an impossibility. In our own case we have divided our efforts among all the house plants and can claim no expertise on the subject. But we do know enough to be astonished at some of the recommendations made by experts to amateurs. It is as if they were more desirous of showing off their own knowledge than of helping the beginner, for most of their choices are difficult to come by, difficult to grow, or both. A single amateur's success with a plant is no proof of its ease of culture. The several we discuss have been chosen because *many* amateurs working with different clones have had success with them. In the coming years we will discover that great numbers of fine orchids can be relied upon to do well in the house.

These wonderful plants have two distinct drawbacks in cultivation. Most of them have unattractive foliage and are an eyesore in the garden most of the year, and the vast majority bloom only once a year. Anything can throw them off—wrong temperatures, lack of a temperature drop to initiate buds, aerial pollution, watering at the wrong time, fungus and virus diseases. In spite of this, we all want to grow orchids if we can. Costliness is being partly overcome by the commercial meristem method of tissue propagation, which speeds up the process immeasurably.

Orchids which grow in the ground have roots and leaves similar to other plants. Tree-growing orchids (epiphytes) have thick aerial roots and erect oval or canelike bulbs called pseudobulbs. Out of these grow one or more leaves. Flower sprays arise either from the base of the pseudobulb or from its top. These bulbs are annual growths. Blooming takes place only from new growths. After flowering, the bulbs gradually lose their leaves and serve mainly as supplementary water and food storage for new pseudobulbs. In this condition they are called "back bulbs." When dividing an orchid plant, we separate into sets old back bulbs and new pseudobulbs so that, in each instance, the new growth has one or more back bulbs in reserve. Usually each pseudobulb, after flowering, produces two new pseudobulbs, one on each side.

Terrestrial orchids (ground orchids) are grown in a highly organic soil. You would be well advised to buy terrestrial mix from an orchid nursery rather than mix your own. Epiphytic orchids use a number of different organic mixes as soil. Again, it is best to purchase epiphytic fir bark mix from an orchid nursery. All orchids require yearly repotting, and most experts consider early spring to be the best time for doing it. This is one instance in which we depart from our house plant rule of not using crock. Orchids require such perfect aeration for their roots that a thick layer of crock in the bottom of the pot is advisable. In the house, plastic pots are to be preferred to clay. To give the epiphytic orchids good aeration at the roots, it pays to burn holes into the pot halfway down large enough to show the mix inside.

The best orchids for the house are those listed in the catalogues as "warm-growing." Contrary to the popular notion, great numbers of the best species require cool temperatures well below normal house levels throughout the year. Those we have chosen will do their best at temperatures no higher than eighty degrees F. A coolish cellar or an air-conditioned room are therefore satisfactory. On hot summer days, they may suffer in the uncooled house or apartment. At such times moving air is a must and a fan is required.

Almost all orchids need humidity of over fifty percent. Trays with pebbles or plastic crate or a humidifier will provide it.

Watering can be continuous throughout the year, but the plants should never stand in it. During and after blooming and until new shoots appear, water should be withheld. Misting, however, is always beneficial. Never allow water to collect in the base of the leaves.

Most orchids will not tolerate direct summer sunlight, especially through glass. At that time of year set them at the side or farther back. Under the lights, their requirements vary. A distance of six to twelve inches is usually satisfactory.

Most orchids like an acid medium (some Slipper Orchids are an exception) and should be fertilized once a week with a high-nitrogen formula. Aerial and underground roots are very sensitive. Once a month allow water from the faucet to run through the pots to leach out the salts.

Other pointers turn up in our descriptions of the various plants. If you take special care at the beginning and get to know the characteristics of these unusual plants, you will have tremendous fun growing them.

◄ *Brassavola nodosa. Orchidaceae.*   Central America. Lady of the Night. Good beginner's orchid for windowsill or light garden.

Buy for bloom in spring
HEIGHT: 10 inches
COLOR OF BLOOM: white and yellow
HABIT: erect quilled leaves
LIGHT: partial sun
TEMPERATURE: minimum 55 degrees F.
MOISTURE: just moist
PROPAGATION: division

Orchids of the same species which grow in different areas often are also different in appearance and in culture. The geographical range of some of the species is very great, and it is often hard to generalize about their behavior. A plant that comes from a higher elevation looks and behaves differently than one from the seashore. Once the wildlings have been grown in greenhouses for a while, raised from seed, and selected they often acquire recognizable characteristics which we can count on.

Brassavola nodosa is a beautiful orchid which is easy to grow. But make no mistake: floriferousness, flower size and shape, and rapidity of growth depend on the plant you happen to own. The best clones are excellent house plants.

The leaves are dark green, channeled, thick quills up to ten inches high, and seeming to grow out of a mass of white aerial roots. In some varieties they are much shorter. The flower stalk emerges from a sheath partway up the leaf and bears several flowers which vary in size from three to five inches in diameter. The lip is a white heart shape at the end of a tube, and the tepals (petals and sepals) are long, narrow and yellow. This doesn't sound too auspicious, but the bloom is very shapely, and when a spray with three or four flowers is on the go, the effect is magnificent. Any one of the new pseudobulbs may produce flowers at any time of the year and a big plant may almost always be in bloom. The flowers last a couple of weeks at least. The fragrance, which is only detectable at night, is delicious. Some hybrids with *Epidendrums* have pink lips or speckled ones but they seem to lack the aristocratic qualities of the original.

B. nodosa grows in orchid bark mix, which can be kept tolerably moist throughout the year. As usual with orchids, spring is a good time to pull the plant out of the pot, shake off the old mix, cut off any dead roots and repot. It produces quantities of aerial roots, which can be partly buried when repotting. As the roots and aerial roots of all orchids are very brittle, pot them tenderly, not pressing directly down into the pot but working the mix inward from the wall of the pot by means of a stick or any blunt tapered instrument. As you work toward the center you can fill in at the sides.

Brassavola likes a bright exposure without full midday sun, especially through glass. Under the lights, place it as much as a foot away. Fertilize regularly and spray in the morning. Once every couple of months leach out the pot by running lukewarm water through it. Even a small pot may have a lot of leaves and be putting up new ones at all seasons of the year.

Catasetum. Orchidaceae. Tropical America. Warm-growing, seasonally blooming orchids for window or light garden.

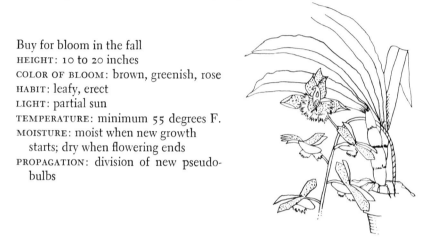

Buy for bloom in the fall
HEIGHT: 10 to 20 inches
COLOR OF BLOOM: brown, greenish, rose
HABIT: leafy, erect
LIGHT: partial sun
TEMPERATURE: minimum 55 degrees F.
MOISTURE: moist when new growth starts; dry when flowering ends
PROPAGATION: division of new pseudobulbs

Catasetums have thick spindle-shaped pseudobulbs and wide, long leaves. The flowering stem dangles and bears long-lasting blooms two to five inches in size. In nature, extraordinarily dissimilar male and female flowers are found on the same plant in most species. The males are the handsomer type and the only ones which will appear on your plant indoors.

To anyone familiar only with corsage orchids these flowers, as well as some of the many other botanical orchids, will be an eye-opener. The shapes and colors are like no other flowers, and the Catasetums in particular have a unique characteristic. Arching out above the lip is the column, which, as in all orchids, embodies the pollination organs. Dangling from the column are two triggers. When disturbed by a visiting bee, the triggers cause a cap over the anthers to pop off, and the former are ejected violently smack on the back of the insect to which they adhere while the visitor flies off to a female flower and pollinates it. You have to see Catasetums to believe them.

166

The most gorgeous of these and the one with the largest flowers is C. *pileatum* with waxy white or yellow blooms. Two other adaptable species with variable and exciting flowers are C. *fimbriatum* and C. *saccatum*. C. *roseum* is also amenable to indoor culture.

Catasetums bloom from winter to early spring, after which the leaves deteriorate. At this time, withhold water and put aside the pot until new growth appears. If there is more than one pseudobulb, separate them and pot up each in ordinary orchid bark mix. The pot should be only a little wider than the pseudobulb, as for bulb plants. Be careful to set the pseudobulb at the same level as before, with the mix reaching just to the bottom of the bulb.

As new growth develops, water freely and fertilize with a high-nitrogen solution once every two weeks. Apply the fertilizer only after moistening the medium. Very light, frequent mistings do these plants good but must be gentle.

Place the pots in brightest indirect light or with the tip of the pseudobulb just below the tubes. As the leaves develop, the pot must be lowered so that the leaves are always two inches away from the lamps. Do not turn the plant in raising or lowering it, but give it the same angle at all times. Do not disturb it in the window.

House temperatures are satisfactory, but a humidity of fifty percent or better is advisable, else the leaves will brown and curl.

The leaves will grow twelve to eighteen inches long and arch over enough to be manageable under lights. The flowering stalk emerges from the base of the pseudobulb. Now support the pot with another— one six or eight inches tall will do—with the stem facing in the same direction as at emergence.

The flowering stem will hang down the side of the pot and bloom fantastically for a number of weeks. During the growth period one or more new pseudobulbs will develop.

• *Epidendrum cochleatum. Orchidaceae.* American tropics. Clam Shell Orchid. Easy orchid for window or light garden. Seasonal bloomer.

Buy for bloom when new pseudobulbs
   are mature or in bud
HEIGHT: 12 inches
COLOR OF BLOOM: dark maroon and
   yellow
HABIT: leafy, erect
LIGHT: partial sun
TEMPERATURE: minimum 55 degrees F.
MOISTURE: even moisture
PROPAGATION: division of pseudobulbs

The lip of an orchid, often its largest and most distinguishing feature, usually points downward. It is an upside-down flower because this feature, which is really an enlarged petal, belongs on top, and in the bud, that is where it is. But as the flower opens it makes a one hundred and eighty degree turn, landing on its head. *Epidendrum cochleatum* is an upside-down orchid, for its lip is on top and the tepals hang down. In some orchids—and this *Epidendrum* may be one of them—it arrives there as the result of a three hundred and sixty degree journey. Who said nature isn't wonderful?

The "clam shell" is the lip, which is striped purple; the tepals* are yellow. To us it looks more like an octopus. Three inches long, this is an oddly showy flower that grows on the end of stems arising from ovoid pseudobulbs with a plume of leaves. The height of a plant may range from eight to fifteen inches. Bloom is in late winter, and long-lasting.

Treat it like *Oncidium ornithorhynchum* (page 175).

---

* The segments of a flower in which both sepals and petals are equally showy are called tepals.

• *Epidendrum radicans. Orchidaceae.* American tropics. Nearly ever-blooming orchid for window or light garden.

Buy for bloom at any time
HEIGHT: 2 feet in the house
COLOR OF BLOOM: cinnabar, orange
   and yellow
HABIT: long canes
LIGHT: full sun in city
TEMPERATURE: minimum 50 degrees F.
MOISTURE: evenly moist
PROPAGATION: separate the canes or
   pot up kcikis (growths on stems)

At orchid nurseries, one plant which always seems to be in bloom. In some corner, out of the way of the collector's items, you will see canes rising to the roof topped with clusters of small flowers in a number of brilliant colors. These are *Epidendrum radicans, E. ibaguense,* or *E.* 'O'Brienianum', the last a hybrid between *E. erectum* and *E. radicans.* The single long stems are lined partway with alternate short fleshy leaves. The rest is naked, and at the top is a closely packed cluster of one-inch flowers with five tepals and a beautiful, complex, fringed and spotted lip. The colors are dominated by *radicans* and *ibaguense,* the tepals being orange or cinnabar and the lip yellow. In 'O'Brienianum' and variations there are also pinkish and purplish shades. The tip of the cane constantly produces more buds and flowers until the stem becomes woody. New canes develop from the base and from growths (keikis) on the stem itself which develop leaves and roots and can be separated and potted up. Don't be in any hurry to remove the old cane as it may bloom more than one season.

Young plants in bloom can be bought, no more than fifteen inches high, in six-inch pots and planted in ordinary fir bark orchid mix. Place them in bright reflected light in the country, and full sun in the city. Under the lights we set them on the edge of the light garden with the pot tilted so that the cane tip is three or four inches under the tubes. Water and fertilize regularly with high-nitrate formula, mist often, and you will have many months of bloom. High humidity is, of course, beneficial. The new canes grow quite rapidly and provide the next year's bloom.

* *Laelio-cattleya* 'Rojo'. *Orchidaceae.* Hybrid. An example of a type of orchid which does well on windowsill or under lights.

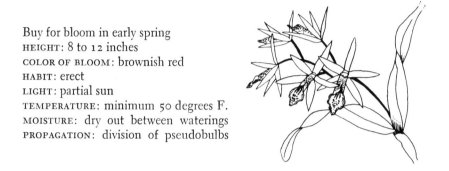

Buy for bloom in early spring
HEIGHT: 8 to 12 inches
COLOR OF BLOOM: brownish red
HABIT: erect
LIGHT: partial sun
TEMPERATURE: minimum 50 degrees F.
MOISTURE: dry out between waterings
PROPAGATION: division of pseudobulbs

The orchid species *Cattleya, Laelia, Epidendrum* and *Brassavola,* plus others—all from Central and South America—are so closely related that it has been possible to cross many of the species. The result is that there is a myriad of plants available on the market with blooms and growth ranging in size from dwarfs to the huge corsage type. In this welter of choices the indoor grower is very much on his own. People who have greenhouses can, because of space and conditions, try a great number of these plants and keep the best of them. But the indoor grower must try to make a good choice the first time out. He gets very little help in this respect from the experts. His only hope is to be well advised by a nurseryman familiar with indoor growing conditions.

Lc. 'Rojo' is an example of a member of this complex particularly suited to windowsill and light garden growth because it is very compact and has beautiful, long-lasting three-inch flowers, several to a spike. Two bloomings a year are not unusual. This particular hybrid is not new and has been superseded by dozens of others equal or better. We speak of it because it has been neglected in our light garden for the last five years and has been a sterling performer nevertheless. The color of 'Rojo' is a true rich, almost brownish red—superior in our opinion to the regular *Cattleya* reds which always have a rather insipid bluish tinge.

We pot 'Rojo' in a two-and-a-half-inch square pot with a regular orchid bark mix supplied by the nursery. The moistened medium is worked in toward the plant from the sides by leverage with a blunt instrument so that it is very compacted. 'Rojo' grows only six inches high, so there is plenty of room for four pseudobulbs and two to four new growths.

We keep plants both on the windowsill and under lights, and they seem to do equally well in either location. In the window they get western sunlight in the spring and summer and are switched to a southern exposure in winter. Normal house temperatures agree with them much better than with most Cattleyas, which require cooler temperatures. The humidity is generally 50 percent or better, and we keep the plants moist all through the year and fertilize them with a higher-nitrate formula or whatever else we are using for our other flowering plants. We really cannot make distinctions for the few orchid plants in our general collection so this one takes what it gets. We do mist the plant occasionally and are careful not to pour water on the leaves.

In March it sends up a sheath which looks as if it will never bloom. It turns from green to light tan, and when this happens, if we see that growth inside has not reached the tip, we cut the last quarter inch off with a scissors. In late April or May the spike emerges with its cluster of buds, and a few weeks later the bloom starts and lasts for eight weeks. Following bloom, if there is room for new growth in the pot we leave it alone and carry on as usual. But if the pot is really crowded we decant the plant, remove the old medium carefully from the brittle roots, break it apart into an approximately equal number of pseudobulbs and now have two two-and-a-half-inch pots of 'Rojo'. For the first weeks after repotting we go easy on watering but do more misting. Then, if we see that the new growths are lengthening we resume normal watering and fertilizing.

Orchids of this type are often called "Cocktail Orchids." We find them very satisfactory and much prettier in the house than the huge floppy things grown for corsages. But if you should cut off one of the flowers in its prime and make a corsage of it, in our opinion the result is far more handsome and unusual. Because of its small size this type of orchid plant can be grown indoors in greater numbers than the larger plants. And, since hybrids can be found which bloom at different seasons

171

of the year, you can have a continuous blooming from your Laelio-cattleyas alone. We must also repeat that since orchid foliage is among the ugliest in the plant world (at least most of the popular blooming types), the smaller plants will at least occupy a smaller area of ugliness than the big ones and are much more likely to have some flowers showing to convert the Beast into a real Beauty.

• *Lockhartia oerstedii. Orchidaceae.* Central America. Braided Orchid. Windowsill, light garden and terrarium. Chronic bloomer.

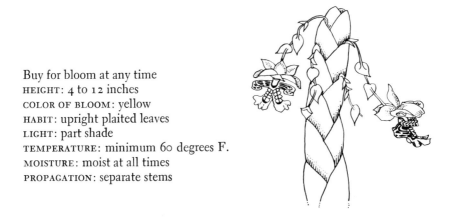

Buy for bloom at any time
HEIGHT: 4 to 12 inches
COLOR OF BLOOM: yellow
HABIT: upright plaited leaves
LIGHT: part shade
TEMPERATURE: minimum 60 degrees F.
MOISTURE: moist at all times
PROPAGATION: separate stems

Not long ago a friend asked us for an orchid likely to do well in a bottle garden. On impulse we broke apart a plant of *L. oerstedii*, which was about four inches high, and gave one part to him. About eight months later he turned up with a glass jug about fifteen inches high. Within it our little *Lockhartia* had become a monster plant knocking against the top of the bottle and loaded with dozens of complex little yellow flowers. His problem was to get it out of the bottle and he had just about decided to cut the glass to get at the plant. The orchid had grown fantastically in a bed of moist sphagnum moss in a closed atmosphere with relatively little light. You might try this yourself in a large bottle or terrarium.

The Lockhartias are small plants with stems consisting of braided leaves. The flowers explode from the cracks in the braiding on threadlike stems. They are about three quarters of an inch long, yellow and similar in their complexity to the flowers of Oncidiums. Each flower lasts for many days. New stems are constantly starting up, and thus a healthy growing plant is in bloom on and off throughout the year. When you want to start a colony, just pull groups of the leaf stems apart along with the root at their bases.

A two- or three-inch pot is quite sufficient and osmunda fiber or sphagnum moss will do as a medium. They like lots of humidity, warm temperatures and very moderate lighting. Even in a window we would recommend enclosing the plant in a terrarium and setting it where it will not receive the full rays of the sun. If planted in osmunda no fertilizer is required, and in sphagnum only the mildest of solutions once a month. Lockhartia does well on the open shelf of your light garden if kept moist and misted daily. But even there a terrarium is preferable.

This is an attractive and easy plant, and when it is in full bloom it is an enchanting sight.

Miltonia spectabilis **and hybrids.** *Orchidaceae.* Central America. Pansy Orchid. Windowsill and light garden. Seasonal bloomer (winter).

Buy for bloom in the fall
HEIGHT: 10 to 20 inches
COLOR OF BLOOM: deep pink and white
HABIT: leafy, erect
LIGHT: bright reflected
TEMPERATURE: minimum 60 degrees F.
MOISTURE: moist at all times
PROPAGATION: division of pseudobulbs

Although all Miltonias are called Pansy Orchids, only M. *vexillaria* and its forms and hybrids really deserve the name. These are enormous, brilliant, flattened flowers on rather small plants, which are still difficult to grow indoors. *M. spectabilis*, however, is a larger plant with a smaller, but still large flower, and it grows like a weed with little care.

Orchids are the most variable of plants and our *Miltonia* is no exception. The flowers, which are about three inches across, have a pink lip and roseate or white petals. Variations run to browns and pinks. Hybrids run the gamut. That with *M. regnellii* is particularly vigorous.

The narrow oval pseudobulbs are six inches long and the narrow leaves eight to ten inches. Sprays come out from either side of a new pseudobulb and bear from four to eight flowers in succession over several weeks, usually in midwinter.

Miltonia should be potted up in regular orchid bark mix, watered regularly throughout the year and fertilized with high-nitrogen fertilizer until spikes appear, when a high-phosphate fertilizer is helpful. The plant prefers over fifty percent humidity but doesn't need it and will flourish at the side of a window or outside the light garden looking in. In the better hybrids and selected plants of the species growth is continuous, new shoots appearing almost immediately following bloom. Soon the plant fills a large pot and has to be divided.

The *M. spectabilis* hybrids are fairly indifferent to temperatures in the house. They don't even require any organic material to grow on. We have raised them successfully in porous slag and gravel.

Dividing the plant is a simple process of cutting apart at least one recent pseudobulb and one back bulb. But since each healthy new pseudobulb produces two more, the effect is much finer if you have a number of pseudobulbs doubling themselves and each of the new ones sending up two sprays. Then it really becomes a show plant in a ten-inch azalea pot.

Miltonias of this type seem little subject to fungal or insect infections. If the leaves start to brown in contact with the tubes, just cut them neatly back with a scissors and the plant will be no worse for wear.

On the whole, these are among the easiest of the orchids to grow, maintain and bloom.

• ***Oncidium ornithorhynchum. Orchidaceae.*** Central America. Windowsill or light garden. Can be grown in a terrarium. Seasonal bloom.

Buy for bloom in the spring
HEIGHT: 12 inches
COLOR OF BLOOM: pink
HABIT: leafy, erect
LIGHT: bright reflected
TEMPERATURE: minimum 60 degrees F.;
    maximum 85 degrees
MOISTURE: moist except dryish after
    bloom until new growth appears
PROPAGATION: divide pseudobulbs

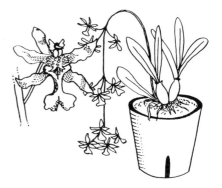

Oncidium ornithorhynchum (the *ch* is pronounced K) flowers are pink except for a touch of yellow in the center. It has two- to three-inch fat oval pseudobulbs and eight- to ten-inch leaves. Sprays are produced from the sides of the bulbs on very wiry stems and bear a large number of very complex half-inch flowers. Examine them under a magnifying glass. They are really something. The odor at certain times of day is very powerful—variously described as sweet or rank. I would say it is a combination of both. Contrary to the popular notion, many orchids are fragrant, while others have an aroma which will knock you over. We once came across a colony of six little ground orchids in the Catskills which smelled so strongly of vanilla that they were noticeable fifty feet away.

The culture of *O. ornithorhynchum* is almost the same as for *Miltonia* except that, after flowering, the plant should only be misted until new shoots appear—whereupon watering and feeding can start up again. It is a midwinter bloomer but has been known to perform twice a year. Flowers last for a couple of months. Keep the top of the plant within five inches of the lights when in growth, but move it away when it starts to bloom, as the flowers will last longer. In the window bright but not burning sunlight is advisable. Division is as for *Miltonia.* This orchid is not expensive and it will give you pleasure for years.

Like so many other orchids, this one does not like to have water in the joints of the leaves, nor should the leaves be moist after dark. Water early in the morning when possible and mist often. If black tips develop, spray with Benlate.

· **Paphiopedilum. Orchidaceae.** East Asia. Slipper Orchids. Seasonal bloomers for windowsill and light garden.

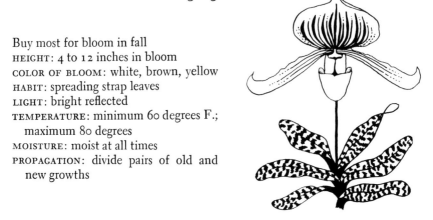

Buy most for bloom in fall
HEIGHT: 4 to 12 inches in bloom
COLOR OF BLOOM: white, brown, yellow
HABIT: spreading strap leaves
LIGHT: bright reflected
TEMPERATURE: minimum 60 degrees F.;
   maximum 80 degrees
MOISTURE: moist at all times
PROPAGATION: divide pairs of old and
   new growths

The Slipper Orchids are ideal ones to begin with, either on the windowsill or under lights, if you try the warm-growing types first. For these terrestrials are grouped according to their temperature requirements. Most of the warm growers can be identified by their spotted or marbled foliage, while the cool ones are shiny dark green. Also, most of our warm growers are species, and the cool ones are those which have been hybridized to produce numerous forms.

The warm-growing plants to consider are P. *bellatulum, callosum, concolor, curtisii, delenatii, godefroyae, laurenceanum, mastersianum, niveum, rothschildianum* and *sukhakuli*. Most of these are small plants whose flower stems do not grow over six inches and whose spread is no more than ten inches.

If you are a beginner, it is not wise to make up your own terrestrial mix. In the catalogues of orchid nurseries you will find "Terrestrial Mix" listed. Order that and you will be much surer of results. Do not, by mistake, order epiphytic mix, which consists of fir bark or chips. Terrestrial orchids grow in the ground and require more finely divided and richer material.

The second consideration is temperature. Warm-growing Paphs

(for short) like a night temperature of fifty-five to sixty degrees F. and a day temperature of seventy to eighty degrees. What this means is that you must guard against temperatures over eighty degrees. An air-conditioned apartment is just about ideal. In the country good ventilation helps, but a hot city apartment is lethal.

Paphs prefer high humidity—over fifty percent—and should be misted, not sprayed.

As for light, they are sometimes rated as requiring as much as two thousand footcandles. This is nonsense. You are more likely to over- than underlight these plants. They will do just fine under two forty-watt fluorescent tubes or in an east window away from direct sunlight. The smaller plants will bloom in a good-size terrarium at a distance of a foot or more from two twenty-watt lamps.

Paphiopedilums should be moist at all times but not soaked. Water the medium, not the plants. The moment water gathers in the axils of the leaves, they are subject to rapid fungal infection, with loss of the whole plant. This is your greatest danger.

Warm-growing Paphs are less acid in their demands than most orchids. Some—the small grayish types—even enjoy a bath of limey water. A balanced fertilizer is best and should be used monthly at standard dilutions.

Given these conditions, the plants will usually bloom sometime in the fall through early spring, the flowers lasting for a month or more. Some will even bloom twice in a year.

One hybrid we have not mentioned in the group is P. 'Maudiae' (callosum x lawrenceanum). This very popular slipper orchid with mottled foliage and white-and-green-striped large flowers is a favorite. It often blooms twice annually, and its only drawback, at least for the light garden, is that it is a rather tall plant—over fifteen inches when in bloom.

The cool-growing, green-leaved hybrids have larger flowers than the warm. Typical are those with mahogany slippers and a huge upper petal, white-spotted with brown or red. But there are yellows-and-whites too. Hybridizers are also working on a pinkish shade which is very attractive. The plants are larger (leaves are a foot long) and the flowers are of very heavy substance.

Culture of the cool Paphs is the same as for the warm-growing orchids except for that factor of temperature. The range is fifty degrees to seventy-five degrees F. Certain of the hybrids require continuous coolness. Others are more tolerant and will do well in an air-conditioned room. Since the situation regarding hybridization is rather analogous to that of African Violets picking out particular ones is difficult for the amateur. So you must throw yourself on the mercy of a good orchid grower for advice. If you inform the nursery of your needs, it will usually ship a satisfactory plant.

A good indicator is the growing of one friend in an air-conditioned apartment. The orchids are on shelves and a room humidifier faces them during the day. At night the machine is rolled into a closet if there are guests. The Paphs all bloom well. But, remember, there will be many months when they will not flower and other plants will have to fill in.

• *Phalaenopsis. Orchidaceae.* East Indies. Moth Orchids. Warm-growing orchids for window and light garden. Long blooming season.

Buy in early spring for bloom
HEIGHT: in bloom to 30 inches. Spread
    8 to 24 inches
COLOR OF BLOOM: white, pink, striped
HABIT: spreading strap leaves
LIGHT: bright reflected
TEMPERATURE: minimum 65 degrees F.
    to maximum 90 degrees
MOISTURE: moist at all times
PROPAGATION: see text below

Phalaenopsis are ideal plants for growing in the house except for their sensitivity to aerial pollution and the great spread of some of the plants. As to the first, you can only hope that your local pollution will decrease as the ecological movement gains momentum. Fortunately, many of the new hybrids are smaller plants—which takes care of the second objection. For years the only objective of orchid breeders was to produce bigger and bigger plants with bigger flowers (with "good" form of course, as defined

178

by the orchid hierarchy). Now, having reached some sort of dead end, the trend is toward more interesting shapes and colorations, which is all to the good. And since the species used in these crosses are usually smaller than the earlier ones, the resultant plants are also more compact.

Moth Orchids grow in long, very often branched sprays. The flowers, ranging in size from one-and-a-half to four inches across, are broad rather than long, looking a bit like an old-fashioned dress bow tie. The lateral petals are very broad, the sepals—one above, one on each side of the lip below—are narrower. Short and pendant from the center of the flower is the lip, which varies considerably but usually looks rather like a head in the center of the flower with two arms outstretched or curved upward, a fat body and two skinny legs turned upward. Sometimes the legs are absent. Old-style Phalaenopsis were principally white or pink with colored or spotted lips. The new hybrids often have stripes running across the tepals and many other types of markings. None of the orchids have clearer colors—either pastel shades or lacquered effects. One large spray of these marvelous flowers seems to dance in the slightest movement of air.

How the non-orchid specialist can be expected to make a satisfactory choice from the catalogues of the nurseries we do not know. The eventual size of the plant is never indicated, to say nothing of suitability for indoor growing, resistance to disease and pollution and general vigor. Even the orchid fancier is engaged in a constant gamble analogous to the hit-or-miss choosing among African Violets. As mentioned elsewhere, in the matter of orchids the newcomer must throw himself on the mercy of the nurseryman who, if he is knowledgeable and honest, will provide you with a suitable plant. Tell him your growing conditions and desires and he may oblige.

Generally speaking, species and the new hybrids between species *Phalaenopsis* are the best for indoor growing. The petals of the flowers are narrower and are often spotted or lined with contrasting colors. To our taste these yellows, pinks and violets with all kinds of markings are far more beautiful and aristocratic than the featureless old-style heavy blooms.

Phalaenopsis is a monopodial genus—meaning that it grows from a single stem. The broad strap leaves of heavy texture curve out from it and the growth is slow. The spike appears from the axils of the leaves and becomes anywhere from fifteen to thirty inches long, depending on the plant. The flowers are very long-lasting and the spike should never be cut after the first flowering, for, in a healthy plant, branches will soon appear and these will also bloom, making it quite possible for a plant to be in flower for six to nine months of the year. No other orchids quite compare with it in this respect and few plants can match its beauty and variety.

The Moth Orchid combines low light requirements with a tolerance of warmer temperatures (seventy to ninety degrees F.) than most others. In the window it should never have direct sunlight and under the lights it can be placed at either end of the tubes or a foot below the center. In the light garden, when the flowering spike develops, the plant can be moved out from under the lights, with only the spike reaching in.

Culture is really very simple. There are just two don'ts: Never get water on the leaves and never let the plant dry out completely. We can prevent the first by always watering the medium, not the plant, and the second by keeping the plant constantly moist. Drainage should be perfect and the pot must never stand in water.

Phalaenopsis needs plenty of room for its roots. It produces both soil and aerial roots. The latter will attach themselves to the outside of clay pots as if they were cemented on. A small plant requires a six-inch pot, and a large bloomer, even of the modern smaller plants, must have an eight- to twelve-incher. Potbinding will inhibit bloom.

You will usually buy your *Phalaenopsis* as a young plant, perhaps ready to have its first flowering, already potted up in medium orchid bark mix. Water thoroughly when the surface appears dry. Fertilize once a month with high-nitrate solution until a spike appears, and then switch to high phosphate-potash fertilizer. High humidity is very beneficial but you can substitute frequent misting, being careful not to build up enough moisture on the leaves to collect in the axils. Most of these plants are winter or spring bloomers, although some may put up spikes at any time of the year.

Eventually your plant may become completely overgrown—so tall that it flops, and so full of root that it is unmanageable. There are ways of perpetuating it but they are for the specialists and should be studied in the books, or the job done by a friendly nurseryman. Occasionally the stem will develop a young plant with roots on the side. This can be broken off and potted up separately. It is also possible to air-layer the plant. But generally speaking, if you have had several years of happiness with the plant it is better to get another one and start over again.

Oh, yes, don't forget to keep these orchids warm. Sixty-five degrees F. and up is what they want.

◢ ***Oxalis regnellii*** **and** ***O. martiana aureo-reticulata.*** ***Oxalidaceae.*** Oxalis. Tropical America. Window and light garden. Everblooming.

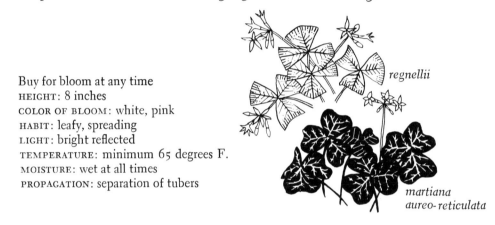

Buy for bloom at any time
HEIGHT: 8 inches
COLOR OF BLOOM: white, pink
HABIT: leafy, spreading
LIGHT: bright reflected
TEMPERATURE: minimum 65 degrees F.
MOISTURE: wet at all times
PROPAGATION: separation of tubers

regnellii

martiana aureo-reticulata

Among the indoor flowering plants there is none easier to grow and bloom than *O. regnellii*. It is the perfect beginners' plant and satisfaction is guaranteed.

Of the Oxalis in cultivation, the ones with tubers or pips are generally more floriferous and easier than the fibrous-rooted kinds. But the most attractive and large-flowered of the former all have a period of dormancy. Only *O. regnellii* and *martiana* do not, and are therefore capable of blooming continuously. No plant of *regnellii* has, in fact, been out of bloom for us. *O. martiana* is less reliable. The growth of these two is very similar, although they do not look at all alike.

O. regnellii grows from tuberous pips in the soil; these pips also build themselves into stemlike clusters below the ground. The plant is stemless and the petiole (leaf stem) grows directly out of the soil some six inches high bearing a single leaf consisting of three large triangular (geometrically so) leaflets which are green on top and burgundy red beneath. The peduncle (stem for several flowers) also grows directly out of the pip and produces several narrow-petaled white flowers, which are not showy. Still, a well-grown plant topped with many of these white stars makes a handsome ensemble and different from any other plant you know.

The leaflet of *O. martiana aureo-reticulata* (gold-veined) are heart-shaped and the veining is truly startling. Flowers are dark pink and not large. It, too, is unique in appearance and forms a magnificent mound of foliage chronically topped by the bloom.

A pip or two of either of these Oxalis planted in Rich Mix with lime in a two-inch pot can be placed in any window away from direct sunlight, or about twelve inches from artificial lighting. If it is watered plentifully and continuously and fertilized with a balanced solution, it will grow and bloom. As new tubers are formed and new leaves and flowers appear, the pot will become crowded and you will have to switch to a larger container.

Eventually your plant will have reached the limits of a desirable spread. Then, knock the plant out of the pot, remove the soil, break the tubers apart and toss them into a small plastic container with moist vermiculite, covering them to a depth of half an inch. Keep the medium quite moist and in some light. Shortly they will begin to sprout. Remove the plants as they appear—you can lift them by their stems, as the vermiculite offers no resistance—and pot them up. *O. martiana* pips, being smaller, are produced in greater number. We have had as many as two hundred and fifty from a medium-sized plant.

These Oxalis prefer temperatures over sixty-five degrees but are not particular about humidity. If leaves turn yellow in the center of the plant, there can be two causes—lack of moisture and/or mites. The mites will ruin a plant in a few days, and we have known growers to throw out the pot, thinking that the whole plant was dead. Never discard these Oxalis. They don't die. If mites are the cause of the trouble (examine leaves under a loupe), simply cut off all top growth and dead leaves and immerse pot and plant in a solution of Kelthane. In a few days the plant will have leaves and flowers again—and no mites. Never dry out this plant.

Pentas lanceolata. Rubiaceae.   Tropical Africa. Egyptian Star Cluster.
Easy plants for window or light garden.

Buy for bloom in late spring
HEIGHT: 12 to 15 inches
COLOR OF BLOOM: white, pink, red
HABIT: erect
LIGHT: full sun
TEMPERATURE: minimum 65 degrees F.
MOISTURE: evenly moist
PROPAGATION: seed or cuttings

Pentas produces flat clusters of starry flowers in white, pink and red
rather easily from seed. Germination takes up to twenty days, but the
seedlings are sturdy. Moved to a four-inch pot and placed in a sunny
window or directly under the lights, watered and fertilized regularly,
they will bloom in about six weeks. The only trouble is that the stems are
rather long and weak (twelve inches or more) so that the flower heads
pull the plant over. Placing them in the brightest light keeps the stems
more sturdy, but a far better method is to grow them, then take cuttings
and start over again. Stems and leaves are both rootable in moist vermiculite at seventy degrees F., and these will usually produce flowers on
short stems. The blooming season is rarely more than about six weeks,
but if you keep cuttings coming along you can have these attractive
flowers all year round.

Plumbago capensis. Plumbaginaceae.   South Africa. Plumbago. Spring-
and summer-blooming viny plant with blue flowers. Window culture.

Buy for bloom in spring
HEIGHT: to 5 feet
COLOR OF BLOOM: blue
HABIT: vining
LIGHT: bright reflected
TEMPERATURE: minimum 60 degrees F.
MOISTURE: evenly moist
TRIMMING: cut back drastically for
    bushiness
PROPAGATION: stem cuttings

The habit of *Plumbago capensis* is well suited to a large sun porch or a corner of a greenhouse but rather disorderly for a window. It has long, thin stems which trail and require tying up on a trellis or other support. Its chief attraction is its light blue phloxlike flowers. These are really a heavenly blue and therefore *Plumbago* is well worth growing.

One absolute requirement is to keep the roots comparatively cool. For this we can only recommend a clay pot and a top layer of sphagnum moss an inch thick kept constantly moist, plus moving air by means of a fan near the pot. Given direct sun in the city, or bright reflected light in the country, the plant will bloom from early spring to fall.

Use plenty of lime in your Rich Mix and water constantly during the summer months. A temperature of sixty-five degrees F. or better encourages bloom. It is also a heavy feeder, and a high phosphate-potash solution is called for. It is a rapid grower and has large roots, hence an ample pot is required. Ten-inchers or a tub may be needed.

In the fall, trim back drastically and reduce watering, but never let the pot dry out completely, and keep in the light. In February repot in new soil. Pieces of stem from newer growth root easily in moist vermiculite. By starting new plants you will avoid having an excessively large one on your hands.

Seed is slow to germinate, taking a month or more, and should be planted below soil level.

Recently we have been growing *Plumbago larpentae* (syn. *Cerato-stigma plumbaginoides*) under lights. This is an erect to trailing plant with wiry branches and rich blue flat flowers in clusters. Although we are not sure as yet, we think this will prove to be a fine addition to the house plant repertory. Keep rather cooler than *P. capensis* but otherwise much the same.

• **Portulaca. Portulacaceae.** Brazil. Will bloom in the light garden or on the windowsill with supplementary light.

Buy for bloom in late spring
HEIGHT: 4 inches
COLOR OF BLOOM: yellow, red, white, pink
HABIT: erect to creeping
LIGHT: full sun
TEMPERATURE: minimum 60 degrees F.
MOISTURE: dry between waterings
TRIMMING: cut back stems to branch
PROPAGATION: stem cuttings and seed; seed any time

The flowers of *Portulaca* come in such a great range of brilliant colors and are so large in relation to their low growth that we are sure you would agree that it would be fun to grow them indoors. However it certainly seems to be an impossible feat since we associate it with sandy soil and the sunniest portion in the outdoor garden. Well, in fact, you can. The light that it requires turns out to be not so much a matter of intensity as of duration. Have it in the window, by all means, but give it the extra hours of supplemental light which will match the sixteen hours it would get in the light garden.

Your first thought will be that it sprawls in an unsightly way—and so it does. You will find, however, that indoors the flowers become much more important than they are in the garden, where the scale of plants is quite different. Portulacas are so colorful that you will tolerate their habit. In winter they bring summer into the home.

Sow seeds of the double mixture in August, and by October your plants will be in bloom. Germination takes ten to fifteen days. Transplant the seedlings two to a two-inch pot and four to a four-inch pot, using Light Mix. Place in the sunniest window position or within four inches of the lights. The first stem will bloom several times directly from the top. Nip it off at the tip and it will start to branch. By judicious pruning you can keep the plant quite compact. Use balanced fertilizer and water moderately. Home temperature ranges suit it. Its height is no more than six inches at any time.

An interesting phenomenon is the durability of the flowers. Outdoors they last only till sundown. Indoors you can expect them to hang on till about nine P.M. under lights.

When you have several plants going and prefer certain colors, make top cuttings three inches long and plant in moist vermiculite. The resultant plants are sturdier than those from seed. It is one of the pleasant recent discoveries of indoor gardening that quite a few of the annuals can be propagated by cuttings, thus providing much quicker replacement. Figure a maximum of six months of active blooming for your Portulacas. Try them; they make a great show.

[❛]*Primula. Primulaceae.* Primrose. China. Plants for the cool window or light garden. Winter bloomers.

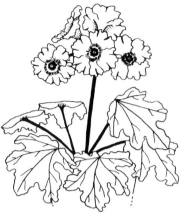

Buy for bloom in the spring
HEIGHT: 6 to 18 inches
COLOR OF BLOOM: pink, white, lilac, red,
    yellow
HABIT: leafy rosette; flowers erect
LIGHT: partial shade
TEMPERATURE: minimum 50 degrees F.;
    maximum 80 degrees
MOISTURE: always moist
PROPAGATION: seed and division

As we have pointed out already, most of the plants recommended for the house prefer a temperature above sixty degrees F. If we can provide cooler conditions the number of possibilities is increased considerably. It just happens that most of us maintain comparatively warm homes and that the majority of the new plants are adaptable to our needs. The cool-growing plant, therefore, however *possible* it may be to grow it, can never be really popular in the house. The reason why so many of this type have been listed in house plant books in the past has been partly because there were more cool sun porches around and partly in a desperate effort to mention a respectable number of plants.

Primroses have been grown in cool greenhouses as winter gift plants, but infrequently from scratch in the house. Light gardening has opened up one interesting possibility—basements frequently have even, rather cool temperatures, and the plants should do well there under fluorescent light. They will also perform on a well-lighted, cool sun porch. In city and country windows, or under artificial light in living areas they are possibilities but difficult. It is not so much room temperature that makes the difference as *root* temperature. Primroses like cool roots. Given that requirement, they may perform, and are certainly worth the effort. There are few lovelier plants.

Three species are suitable for indoor growing: *P. malacoides, P. obconica* and *P. sinensis.* There is also the hybrid *Primula kewensis.* All take very much the same culture. *P. malacoides* is the tallest and has

186

the largest leaves. It is commonly called the Fairy Primrose. Colors are white, rose, lilac. *P. obconica* grows a foot tall and blooms in white, lilac, crimson, salmon. *P. sinensis* is the smallest—eight to ten inches—and blooms in a wide range of colors. This is the plant you usually see in the florist shops, and the popular color is pink. *P. kewensis* grows to eighteen inches and has fragrant yellow flowers.

Plant the seed on top of the soil, as it needs light to germinate. The best time is June for fall and winter blooming. Transplant the seedlings to four-inch pots with Rich Mix containing double the usual amount of added lime. During the growing period the plants must be kept in temperatures less than eighty degrees F. most of the time. Water regularly but do not allow to stand in it. Drainage must be excellent. Never permit it to dry out. Provide humidity of fifty percent and good ventilation. Fertilize once a week in summer with quarter-strength balanced solution and in winter once every two weeks with high phosphate-potash fertilizer. Roots suffer if fertilized excessively. Flowering will start in late fall and continue to the following spring. The temperature in winter should be between fifty and sixty-five degrees F. Bright reflected light in the window and placing plants close to the tubes near the ends will suffice to produce bloom.

Now, assuming that you do not have a cool sun porch or cellar, how can you preserve the low temperatures needed? An air-conditioned room will help considerably in summer. For all year round, and in any warmer position, the following can be tried. Plant the primroses in clay pots. Spray the pots regularly—the evaporation reduces the soil temperature considerably. In addition, pack unmilled coarse sphagnum moss about an inch thick on top of the soil so as to fill the whole space between the rim of the pot and the stem. Spray the moss frequently. This will also produce coolness by evaporation. The addition of a small fan blowing at low level in relation to the plant will also chill. These measures may be successful.

To return to our primroses: *P. malacoides* is an annual. The only special suggestion is to remove flowering stems as they finish blooming. *P. obconica* is a perennial. Handle this one with gloves, as the hairs are irritating to those who are allergic. Repot at the end of the blooming season. *P. sinensis* is treated much the same, but be careful when replanting to set it very high in the pot and support it for the first few weeks by means of a short stake. *P. kewensis* is usually handled as an annual.

• ***Punica granatum nana. Punicaceae.*** Asia. Dwarf Pomegranate. Shrubby plant with wonderful flowers and fruit for window or light garden. Everblooming.

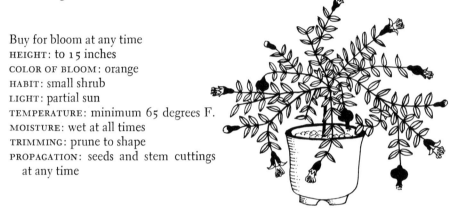

Buy for bloom at any time
HEIGHT: to 15 inches
COLOR OF BLOOM: orange
HABIT: small shrub
LIGHT: partial sun
TEMPERATURE: minimum 65 degrees F.
MOISTURE: wet at all times
TRIMMING: prune to shape
PROPAGATION: seeds and stem cuttings
   at any time

The Dwarf Pomegranate is already very popular among amateur indoor growers and for good reason. It starts blooming when it is only three inches high and just goes on and on from there. The flowers are large for this little shrub, which rarely grows more than fifteen inches in the house, for they are a good one and a half inches long and look like a flaming orange *Fuchsia.* Blow into the flower and a fruit develops which is about an inch and a half in diameter and turns a beautiful "pomegranate" red. The seeds are viable but it is much easier to root young cuttings in vermiculite.

The little tree is very tolerant. Give it Rich Mix with lime, a four-inch pot, good reflected light and regular waterings and fertilizings around the year, and it will be constantly in bloom. Occasionally it rests a bit, then produces startling numbers of buds all at once. If you do set fruit, make it just one at a time as each takes a good deal of strength out of the plant. Temperatures over sixty-five degrees F. and humidity of fifty percent or better encourage growth and bloom.

Punica should be nipped back early in its career so that it bushes out as much as possible. If this is done drastically the plant will develop a thickish trunk and a bushy top or, with more art, you can shape it into a true bonsai. We rate this as among the very best plants for the house.

Rhoeo discolor. Commelinaceae. West Indies. Moses-in-the-Cradle. Amusing plant for windowsill.

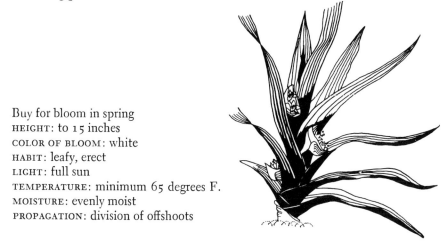

Buy for bloom in spring
HEIGHT: to 15 inches
COLOR OF BLOOM: white
HABIT: leafy, erect
LIGHT: full sun
TEMPERATURE: minimum 65 degrees F.
MOISTURE: evenly moist
PROPAGATION: division of offshoots

Moses-in-the-Cradle is a foliage plant for most of the year and the flowers are inconspicuous. The foliage, dark green above and purple beneath, is attractive but its popularity is, we believe, due more to its common name than anything else, for the blooming period is very short. Flowering takes place near the base of the plant and consists of bracts arranged in an oval like a boat with the small white flowers jammed between the gunwales. *Rhoeo* grows about a foot high.

It requires a six-inch pot of Rich Mix, plenty of water at all times except during cool periods, temperature above sixty-five degrees F., high humidity and occasional feeding. Usually in late spring offshoots develop around the base; these can be potted up separately. Give it as much light as you can—a west or south window.

Roses, Miniature.   Intermittent bloomers for window or light garden.

Buy for bloom at any time
HEIGHT: to 10 inches
COLOR OF BLOOM: pink, white, red
HABIT: erect
LIGHT: sun
TEMPERATURE: minimum 60 degrees F.
MOISTURE: evenly moist
TRIMMING: trim back long stems
PROPAGATION: stem cuttings

For years miniature roses have been sold as house plants on the strength of their beauty and desirability. In practice they have been disappointing. Some of them proved small-flowered all right, but were not dwarf plants. Moved to a larger pot they grew up. Another problem was mite, which turned up regularly and killed off plants within a few days. Some, also, were too hardy for the house, requiring cool temperatures and a semi-dormant period. Even a year ago we were loath to recommend them.

However the picture has changed. The new hybrids are much improved, and the No-Pest Strip takes care of the mites. A few of the novelties are true miniatures and will bloom for you on and off all year long.

Of these hybrids the following may be the best:

- 'Beauty Secret', red flowers and fragrant.
  'Janna', rather large-flowered and shapely. Pink bloom. No scent.
  'Green Ice', tiny, greenish double flowers. Very sturdy.
  'Toy Clown', white with red edge.

These plants seem to be adaptable and responsive to indoor culture. They grow about six inches high. Many other miniature roses do well out-of-doors but they are risky in the house.

Plants from the nursery usually come planted in good garden soil, which seems to suit them. So this is one instance where we don't suggest replanting in mix. Contrary to most of our house plants, roses prefer acid conditions. Allow the soil to dry out partially between waterings and feed with high-nitrate fertilizer every two weeks. Humidity is not important, although they like to be sprayed frequently. Give them full sunlight or a position within five inches of the lights. Ventilation is important. They don't like still air and they flourish with the window partly open in the warm season. However, if the air is sooty, the leaves should be washed frequently, and if the smog gets heavy it is better to shut the window. Cool nights are beneficial, followed by a good spraying in the morning.

Repotting should be done yearly, and when a larger pot is required the extra soil can be Rich Mix without lime.

The mite problem is solved by the No-Pest Strip, and the same treatment can be given for aphids, which also visit these plants. The latter are easily seen. And if your rose develops yellow leaves even though you have been watering it correctly, the chances are that it has mites.

Like all roses, your miniatures should be pruned. Remove the flowers within four days after they have opened as this will encourage the formation of new buds. Cut off a good length of stem—relatively as much as you would with a garden rosebush—for this will encourage new bud formation. In addition, partly cut off unproductive side branches so that the plant will branch more. Try to maintain a symmetrical shape. During the summer you can permit some freedom of growth but, in the fall, trim back sharply as you would any other rose and cut down on watering until the plant shows new growth from all the branches. Then resume regular watering and fertilizing.

Remember that roses are acid-loving plants. They also require a good supply of iron. If leaves become light in color and transparent treat with Sequestrene (chelated iron).

The most successful indoor growers of miniature roses seem to be those who summer the plants outside. This treatment results, apparently, in better blooming during the winter indoors.

• *Schlumbergera, Rhipsalidopsis and Zygocactus* **hybrids.** *Cactaceae.*
Tropical America. Christmas Cactus, Easter Cactus, Thanksgiving
Cactus, etc.

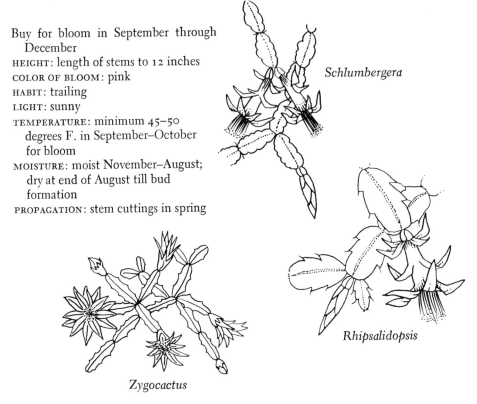

Schlumbergera

Rhipsalidopsis

Zygocactus

Buy for bloom in September through
    December
HEIGHT: length of stems to 12 inches
COLOR OF BLOOM: pink
HABIT: trailing
LIGHT: sunny
TEMPERATURE: minimum 45–50
    degrees F. in September–October
    for bloom
MOISTURE: moist November–August;
    dry at end of August till bud
    formation
PROPAGATION: stem cuttings in spring

We are reluctant to write about plants with which we are uniformly
unsuccessful. We know all the things that should be done and have
occasionally followed instructions with no results. Other people seem
to do nothing and get bloom twice a year. Since we like the plants and
they are undoubtedly beautiful—much more floriferous and long-lasting
than most cacti—we suppose our failures are basically due to an im-
patience with special plant chores when so many of our other blooming
plants do wonderfully without them. Of course nurserymen must get
bloom reliably at particular seasons and for holidays, so there is no
mystery here. And these plants and the more decorative Kalanchoës
just won't bloom unless you follow one of the methods.

Schlumbergera, Rhipsalidopsis and Zygocactus hybrids

The *Rhipsalidopsis* hybrids bloom in the spring, *Zygocactus* around Thanksgiving and *Schlumbergera bridgesii* and *russelliana* at Christmas—more or less. All have the typical long two-layered flowers in pinks and reds. The sections of branch vary in cross section. In the shops you will find them at the appropriate season, usually mislabeled or nonspecific. As they all behave very much the same except for difference of season for bloom you can choose them as you like them.

Sandy soil with some humus suits these cacti, or they can be potted in Light Mix. Real cactus mix is too lean for them. Root systems are small in proportion to the plant and a bit of potbinding does no harm.

From late spring on, water regularly and feed with fish emulsion or a balanced fertilizer once a week. The fun starts in the fall.

The initiation of buds in these cacti is the result of either a cold shock or ten-hour-light days in October for the Thanksgiving type and October and November for the Christmas and spring-flowering kinds. Short day means long night of absolute darkness for fourteen hours. One light bulb burning may spoil your chances of bloom.

This means that you have the easy choice of leaving the plant out of doors until there is danger of frost (or finding some other cool but not freezing place during the period) or you must find some way of cutting down on day length. Obviously this is most difficult in the light garden unless you haul the plant out and stuff it in a closet early each night. In a window garden the days will also be too long. Lucky are those who have an otherwise dark place with a small window providing light for just a few hours every day. Some growers suggest putting the plant in complete darkness for a period—under a black cloth, for instance —but this may not work.

When the "shock" period is over, the plant will start to put out new growth in a sunny window and, with watering, will bloom. This sounds pretty complicated but apparently plenty of people have the right conditions, like a cool sun porch or an enclosed terrace, where they can apply these Spartan methods, for these holiday cacti continue to be popular in a big way. Try them and work on that one problem of providing either a cool or a dark period.

Sections of branch root easily in moist vermiculite if you lay the piece on the surface during the growing period of the plant. Some of the new cultivars are said to bloom both in spring and fall. So, presumably, some of the problems are being overcome, at least in the nursery. For fall bloom you have to give a one-month short-day treatment in August or September followed by a repeat in January.

As postscript we should mention the advice of one experienced grower. She says, just dry them out for a few weeks until they shrivel a bit, then resume watering. The claim is that this will initiate bloom without either the cold shock or the short day.

Scilla violacea. Liliaceae.   South Africa. Small bulb plant for window, light garden or terrarium. Spring bloom.

Buy for bloom in early spring
HEIGHT: to 4 inches
COLOR OF BLOOM: greenish touched
   with purple
HABIT: somewhat spreading.
LIGHT: bright reflected
TEMPERATURE: minimum 60 degrees F.
MOISTURE: dry out between watering
PROPAGATION: division of offsets

Not all of our house plants have gorgeous flowers. The blooms of *Scilla violacea* climb the stem like Lilies of the Valley, but are a modest green touched with purple. However, in the spring, when there are many of them on a small plant, they are quite pretty. The bulbs, which lie on the surface of the soil or partly buried, are purple. The narrow two- to three-inch leaves are beautifully mottled on top in two shades of green, and the reverses are purple, too. It is an extremely neat plant for a small Japanese pot, and when well grown is a gem.

Pot up the bulbs with the bottoms just below the surface of the soil. Water lightly and allow to dry out between waterings. Light Mix is best, with a good admixture of lime. Use a small, decorative pot, or set in the terrarium. Moderate light and normal house temperatures will cause it to grow, put out offset bulbs, and eventually bloom. It's a nice, trouble-free plant.

* **Sonerila margaritacea. Melastomataceae.** Java. Small plant for the warm house in window or light garden.

Buy for bloom in early spring
HEIGHT: to 6 inches
COLOR OF BLOOM: pink
HABIT: leafy, bushy
LIGHT: bright, but partial sun
TEMPERATURE: minimum 65 degrees F.
MOISTURE: evenly moist
PROPAGATION: stem cuttings in high
    humidity and warmth

This is not an easy plant to find at the nurseries and it is a little difficult to grow. We made the mistake twice of failing to protect it against drops in temperature in our plant room. Even sixty degrees is too cool and rot sets in immediately. But the foliage is so beautiful and the small flowers so pretty that it is worth quite an effort.

The complex veining of the two- or three-inch-long leaf is very deep green. In between the veins are irregular areas of pearly white which under some light conditions appears a rich silver. The flowers are four-petaled and deep pink. From the center rises the long, bright yellow cluster of stamens typical of the family. Growth is compact and bushy.

Maintain temperatures of sixty-five degrees F. or better, and give plant high humidity. Pot in Rich Mix and keep just moist. The plant requires bright though not direct sunlight and a position about eight inches under the tubes. Cuttings take easily in moist vermiculite. We have had no experience with insects on this plant. If well grown it is amazingly beautiful.

Spathiphyllum 'Clevelandii', floribundum, etc. *Araceae.* Tropical America. Chronically blooming plants of easiest culture for the window.

Buy for bloom any time
HEIGHT: to 18 inches
COLOR OF BLOOM: white
HABIT: leafy on long stalks
LIGHT: semishade
TEMPERATURE: minimum 65 degrees F.
MOISTURE: evenly moist
PROPAGATION: division

If there is an easier large plant that blooms off and on throughout the year we would like to know about it. Nevertheless, *Spathiphyllum* is not popular with amateurs. Its normal civilized habitat is in a window-box arrangement in some restaurant where it gets a little reflected outdoor light and some supplementary incandescent. Parched and otherwise neglected, it continues to live and bloom with bright white spathes against dark green foliage. The spathe is very much like that of *Anthurium.* We consider it far more attractive than many of the foliage plants we grow in shaded conditions in the house, and more people should have it.

The leaves are long-stalked and spoon-shaped like the spathes. Choose the plants by size. *S. floribundum* has leaves less than a foot in length; some hybrids grow up to two feet or more. 'Clevelandii' is a big tough one. Flower size varies with plant size.

They need nothing more than ordinary soil or Rich Mix, normal house temperatures, regular watering and fertilizing. Light requirements are so low that this is about the only plant which will flower on a coffee table in your living room, provided there are a few hours of bright light flooding it.

The usual insects—scale, mite, etc.—will attack it, but as the leaves are smooth, several washings in water and brown soap will rid it of pests.

The flowers come whenever the plant feels like it; more when it has better light, naturally.

Sprekelia formosissima. Amaryllidaceae. Mexico. St. James Lily. Seasonal bulb for window or light garden.

Buy for bloom in early spring
HEIGHT: 12 inches
COLOR OF BLOOM: crimson
HABIT: erect
LIGHT: full sun
TEMPERATURE: minimum 60 degrees F.
MOISTURE: dry September to February;
   moist February to September
PROPAGATION: offsets

Sprekelia likes bright sun or the best position in the light garden. As with most bulbs, the pot should be close to the lights at first and then dropped gradually as the leaves and flowering stem lengthen. Humidity should be fifty percent or higher.

Pot in Light Mix in February or whenever growth appears at the tip of the bulb, and cover only two thirds of the bulb. Water lightly at first (for a couple of weeks) then increase and keep constantly moist, using balanced fertilizer once a week.

Any time from the end of March to June the crimson, uniquely shaped four-inch flower will bloom. Height of the plant is about a foot. After bloom, the narrow leaves develop more fully until September when the bulb is allowed to dry out; it is then removed from the pot and stored in a warm place (sixty-five degrees F. minimum) till February. Remember: a warm place—for this is one bulb which will not bloom if the temperature drops during its dormancy. Older bulbs produce offsets which can be potted up.

Stapelia variegata. Asclepiadaceae. South Africa. Carrion Flower. Striking succulents for window or light garden. In the latter they bloom on and off throughout the year.

Buy for bloom any time
HEIGHT: to 6 inches
COLOR OF BLOOM: yellow
HABIT: erect to spreading
LIGHT: full sun
TEMPERATURE: minimum 65 degrees F.
MOISTURE: evenly moist; dry when cool
PROPAGATION: division

The Stapelias and the very similar related genera will grow in popularity as they become better known. The flower of S. *variegata* is amazing. From a plant no more than three or four inches high, consisting of angled cactuslike stems, hangs a three-inch flower which is a geometrically perfect flat five-pointed star with a fleshy ring around the middle (annular ring). The color is matte yellow symmetrically daubed with small irregular spots in deep red. It can be grown quite big and the stems *can* grow ten or twelve inches long, but the smaller size is more satisfactory in the house and the dimensions of the flower remain the same.

We have chosen this species because it is at present the most versatile one and the easiest to grow and bloom. For sheer size S. *nobilis* (or *gigantea*) is unbeatable. The stems are a bit longer and heavier than S. *variegata* but the flower, also star-shaped, is a full eleven inches across. The plant is worth growing just for that and for the sight of its big balloon of a bud which takes about a half hour to open fully, each lobe springing free separately.

S. *hirsuta* is another species which grows and blooms well. Its flowers are four to five inches across, purplish and covered with soft long hairs. Many Stapelias and their relatives, the Duvalias, Carallumas and Huernias, are cultivated. Which one will prove a real winner in the future is anybody's guess—all are worth investigating.

The name Carrion Flower is come by honestly. But the odor is not very strong and nobody obliges you to poke your nose into the immediate area. The objectionable feature is not noticeable a couple of feet away except perhaps to a fly, which acts as pollinator, and for whom it is, presumably, infinitely enticing. The odor of good ripe cheese is not exactly Chanel No. 5, but we don't hesitate to eat it. So let the fly have *his* fun and you grow these lovely and easy plants.

Pot small in Cactus and Succulent Mix with plenty of lime. If your plant has arrived very dry from a nursery, merely spray once a day until new growth starts. Then you can begin a regular regimen of plain waterings with a monthly fertilizing of fish emulsion. The pot should not dry out completely if you want the plant to flower regularly. Should you neglect it the stems will shrivel but will recover quickly if lightly watered.

In a sunny window Stapelias will bloom in late summer. Under lights you can get them to perform throughout the year—usually one flower at a time. Humidity is unimportant and the temperature can drop to fifty degrees F. without harming the plant. But for bloom sixty-five degrees F. and over is advisable. Under lights the tips of the stems should be about six inches from the tubes. Oddly enough, they don't like to be too close and will change color and shrivel if they are subjected to too much light. Some species are much more sensitive on this point than others. S. *variegata* requires less light than the others.

The flower bud develops on a dangling stem. So, the moment a bud appears, the pot must be raised up on another pot to give the bud room to grow.

Although regular watering encourages bloom we must warn you that your plant will rot away if it is overwatered. Do not water during cool periods. Do not water if the plant stops growing. If rot develops, it will start at the bottom of the stem. Remove the whole stem, cut off the rotten part up to good green flesh, and follow the procedures for normal propagation.

Propagate Stapelias by stem cuttings. Remove the whole stem from the point where it meets the joining stem. Let it dry out for three days. The end will shrivel. Prepare a pot of Cactus and Succulent Mix, dip the end of each cutting in hormone powder and set it well down in the soil. Place in good light. After a couple of days, start to spray the cutting. Continue with a daily moderate spraying until new growth appears. The process is fairly quick and reliable.

An infestation of mealybugs is possible. Remove those you see with a brush dipped in alcohol (rubbing alcohol will do) and hang a piece of No-Pest Strip in a plastic bag with holes nearby.

Any description of Stapelias is vain. You have to see them. Once seen, you will want to grow them.

Stephanotis floribunda. Asclepiadaceae. Stephanotis. Madagascar. Summer-blooming vine for sun porch or window. Fragrant.

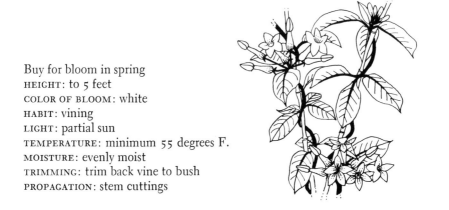

Buy for bloom in spring
HEIGHT: to 5 feet
COLOR OF BLOOM: white
HABIT: vining
LIGHT: partial sun
TEMPERATURE: minimum 55 degrees F.
MOISTURE: evenly moist
TRIMMING: trim back vine to bush
PROPAGATION: stem cuttings

Stephanotis, related to *Stapelia* and *Hoya,* belongs to a group of plants which, in our opinion, is on the wane in popularity. They are old house plants which were particularly successful in the days of cool sun porches. We had one in our suburban home and such plants throve in the bright, filtered sunlight and cool nights there. As gardening moves farther indoors we find ourselves happier with a stinky but magnificently blooming *Stapelia* or any number of other new plants which are neutral or fragrant, and flower throughout the year than with this plant whose season is summer when we are out of the house most of the time—either on vacation or tending our gardens. If we have to have seasonal bloom, then winter is much to be preferred.

Stephanotis, like *Hoya,* is sweet-scented and the flowers are long-lasting. The leaves are thick and shiny and the blooms growing out of the axils remind one of clusters of Trailing Arbutus. Because it's a sturdy vine it must either be trellised or tied to a stake and trained. And, since bloom is from the new young branches, care must be taken to arrange them for maximum visibility of the tubular flowers, which are white, waxy, and one inch long.

The plant does not like the hot sun, but does require some brightness, so it must be placed at the side of the window or somewhat back from the glass. An east window is ideal. It likes cool nights down to fifty-five degrees and doesn't mind hot air during the day as long as it is dry. During spring and summer it is a heavy drinker and should be given a balanced fertilizer once a week. After blooming, in the fall, hold back on moisture and eliminate fertilizing completely. In early spring repot in Rich Mix and possibly a larger pot. Then, too, the plant can be trimmed back if it has grown too rank. The young cuttings take easily in moist vermiculite.

A reason given why *Stephanotis* is often difficult to bloom is that it does not like sudden changes in day temperatures; this seems to inhibit the setting of buds. If you can once get the vine to bloom well, it will supply a long period of enjoyment.

Thunbergia alata. Acanthaceae.   South Africa. Black-eyed Susan Vine. For windowsill or light garden. Easy to grow and bloom under lights but a bit hard to control.

Buy for bloom in spring
HEIGHT: to 5 feet
COLOR OF BLOOM: yellow, black eye
HABIT: weak vine
LIGHT: sun
TEMPERATURE: minimum 65 degrees F.
MOISTURE: evenly moist
TRIMMING: trim back to keep short
PROPAGATION: stem cutting and seed
    at any time

This perennial vine, with its large yellow flowers centered with a startling black spot, grows rapidly from seed, which is available from most seedsmen and germinates in about ten days. Place it on a sunny windowsill, water it aplenty—for it must never dry out—and train it on a fan trellis. Since the stems do not get woody but grow fast, it must be tied up neatly and trained around and around unless you have the place to let it run. As side shoots appear they must be cut off.

A rampant plant, it requires a large pot with Rich Mix and on a windowsill a ten-incher is in order. Give it plenty of balanced fertilizer and temperatures of sixty degrees F. or better. When winter comes it will most likely no longer flower in daylight alone and will require supplementary lighting.

Long days under fluorescent lights agree with it completely and it will bloom all year. The problem is how to keep it in check. Sometimes we just let it grow around the tubes, trimming off excess foliage now and then. Chopped back it is moderately compact, but since it puts out a lot of root, you will still need to move it from a small to a rather large pot under lights. It is such a gay plant that it is worth the trouble. Lucky those who have lights set rather high above the trays and can let it wander a bit.

Thunbergia can be propagated from stem cuttings so that you can keep a new plant coming along all the time. This has its advantages where space is at a premium. But seed responds so well and the packets contain so many of them that this is hardly worth while.

If leaves start to turn yellow in spite of good watering you are in trouble, because this means spider mites of one type or another are probably at work. They particularly like this kind of thin-leaved plant. We suspect that they often come with the seed itself and suggest immersion for a few minutes in a solution of Kelthane before planting. If you already have an infestation, cut back the plant to manageable size and dunk it, pot and all, in a pailful of Kelthane solution. It may recover.

Recently nurseries have been offering *Thunbergia gibsonii*, a stronger vine with larger, vibrant orange flowers. Hence we would not recommend it for a light garden, but it may do very well in a bright, sunny window.

• *Thymophylla tenuiloba. Compositae.* Central America. Dahlberg Daisy. Annual plant which blooms for several months under lights and less reliably in the window.

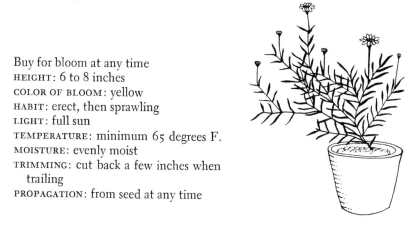

Buy for bloom at any time
HEIGHT: 6 to 8 inches
COLOR OF BLOOM: yellow
HABIT: erect, then sprawling
LIGHT: full sun
TEMPERATURE: minimum 65 degrees F.
MOISTURE: evenly moist
TRIMMING: cut back a few inches when
   trailing
PROPAGATION: from seed at any time

Raise the Dahlberg Daisy from seed (Park Seed Company has it) in a propagation box, transplant to a one-and-a-half-inch pot and then into its permanent home, a two-and-a-half- to three-inch pot, using Light Mix with lime. Water and fertilize regularly. Normal house temperatures are satisfactory.

It is an easy plant and will bloom all winter or summer long, depending on when you have sown the seed, under lights or in the window. Seed germinates in ten days and bloom will start on a single stem when the plant is about a month old.

The flowers are half-inch yellow daisies on top of finest fern foliage. As it develops, the plant branches and becomes a filmy mass so delicate that, in spite of a complete lack of backbone, it does not really interfere with other plants.

The bad habit of the Dahlberg Daisy is easily made up for by its wonderful floriferousness. It is such a sun lover outdoors that it exceeds our expectations when it blooms so easily under lights—even a foot away —or in a sunny window. The one thing we have to do is remove the dead flowers, whose capsules contain seed in enormous quantities. Save the seed and start a new generation. It is the only daisy which is so easy indoors, and the golden color brings sunshine into the winter garden.

• ***Vallota speciosa. Amaryllidaceae.*** Scarborough Lily. South Africa. Bulb plant for the window.

Buy for bloom in August
HEIGHT: 12 inches
COLOR OF BLOOM: red
HABIT: spreading leaves, erect flowers
LIGHT: full sun
TEMPERATURE: minimum 65 degrees F.
MOISTURE: dry after fall blooming till
   February; moist after new growth
   until after boom
PROPAGATION: by offsets

Amaryllis and Lily family flowers are so beautiful that everybody would like to be able to grow them in the house. And, indeed, enthusiastic amateurs manage it. The bulbs of those that need cold weather to initiate bloom are placed in the refrigerator for six to eight weeks and then brought out and grown in the window or under lights. Others which do not need this still have the disadvantage of a short-blooming period and some dormancy. House plant books have always been full of them but we believe that this will subside unless growers manage to develop plants which will compete more effectively with the new, easier, house plants. We include a few, rather shamefacedly, bowing to the tradition. But, with the exception of such a fast-blooming plant as the Amaryllis itself, they are hardly worth the trouble.

Vallota, at least, is rather easy, not too big—about twelve inches high—and has lovely red flowers.

Plant the dormant bulb or young plant, allowing about an inch all around, in Rich Mix with lime. Keep it moist from spring to fall and in full sunlight. Older plants can stand temperatures under sixty-five degrees F. but young ones cannot. Fertilize with balanced mixture once a month. If all is going well, your plant will flower in early fall. Then it wants a dry period until February.

Vinca. Apocynaceae. Asia Minor and the tropics. Periwinkle. Easy plants for window or light garden. Everblooming.

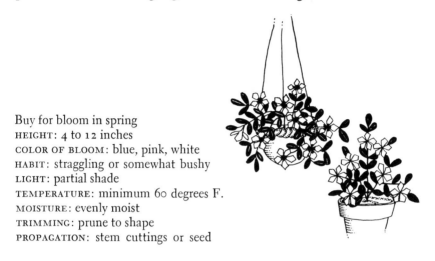

Buy for bloom in spring
HEIGHT: 4 to 12 inches
COLOR OF BLOOM: blue, pink, white
HABIT: straggling or somewhat bushy
LIGHT: partial shade
TEMPERATURE: minimum 60 degrees F.
MOISTURE: evenly moist
TRIMMING: prune to shape
PROPAGATION: stem cuttings or seed

The popular Vincas of borders and shady areas of the garden make good house plants. The flowers, in various shades of blue, pink and white, are somewhat phloxlike, the colors a bit watery. But they are gay and floriferous.

Vinca minor is so common and so much of it has escaped to our roadsides that any trip into the country can procure you a supply of plants. The flowers are a nice blue and up to an inch across. You will find it blooming in shady places where no other showy plant will flower— so it has considerable merit for use indoors. Being a creeper, it must either be kept short in a pot or allowed to hang in a basket.

Pot it hard in Rich Mix without lime and keep moist at all times. It can be well to the side at the window as it requires relatively little light. In the light garden it will bloom at either end of the tubes. Feed occasionally with any fertilizer. It has no special requirements as to humidity and house temperatures, outside of preferring a minimum of sixty degrees F. Of course, if you want a shapely and attractive plant, you have to groom it and check in what location it is happiest under the lights.

There are many forms and cultivars, some bluer than others, and some in white or pink. All the groundcover types are related. 'Polka Dot' (white flowers with a red eye), introduced a few years ago, is part of the complex. Bowle's Variety is larger-flowered.

Vinca major is a bushier plant, growing ten inches high and most often treated as an annual. It comes in many color forms and names, which can be found in the seed catalogues. Culture of these plants is the same as V. *minor* except that they need somewhat more light. Cuttings should be taken and rooted when the Vincas become ratty after a season.

Index

Index

Index